365 Days of Writing Prompts for Romance Writers

Copyright

365 Days of Writing Prompts for Romance Writers

By Kim Knight

Copyright @ Kim Knight 2020

Editing by: Story House Editing

Other books By Kim Knight

Romance Set in Paradise: Havana Heat Book One

Romance Set in Paradise: Lover's Retreat Book Two

The Suspenseful Collection: Volume One (Co-authored with Didi Oviatt)

The Suspenseful Collection Volume Two – Blurred Lines (Co-authored with Didi Oviatt)

Romance in the City: Not Just for Christmas

Romance in the City: The Red Room

Romance in the City: Trust in Me (released end of 2020)

A Stranger in France: Romantic Suspense

Sacrifices: Historical Romantic Suspense (August 2020)

Author Thank You and Dedication

Firstly, I have to thank the romance author Kristi Tailor because it was her surprise reveal and Facebook share of her personal notebook journals that pushed me to get on with my own creative project outside of being a romance author. For a while I've had this idea, '365 days of writing prompts.' If it were not for Kristi tagging me into her launch of her new journals, I probably would still be procrastinating. So, thanks Kristi! Love from Europe.

Secondly, I dedicate this writing reference aid to all writers who love to read, write and create great romance stories. No matter your sub-genre of romance, this is for you! I hope you have a fun year and that I help increase your productivity and creativity.

Chapters

December- Romance Writer's Blog Prompts

Introduction

Welcome! This book of writing prompts is for all my 'tribe' of fellow romance writers, no matter what sub-genre or heat level you represent. I'd love to spend the year with you as you create some great stories. You might be thinking 'well who the hell is this woman, and why has she done this?' Okay, here's the deal. Back in 2016 I crossed paths with a fellow suspense and thriller author, we became wonderful friends and for sure she's a girlfriend for life. Her name is Didi Oviatt, you may know her. Anyway, we went on to start a very simple blogging challenge together where we created short stories of about 2,000-3,000 words each week. One of us would write one half, and the other would finish it. No discussion, planning or anything. The best bit is we used writing prompts voted on by our blog followers and readers. At the time of writing this four years later, we're seventeen stories and two novels deep! We have published them and are currently working on book three. I have also used writing prompts to interact with my followers, readers and fans via my own author site since day one. I love writing prompts, so for me, writing prompts have really helped with creativity, productivity and most importantly building a readership. If it can work for me, friend it can work for you. If you're still curious, my bio is below.

I was born in 1983 I'm from London in the UK. I'm a mother to a beautiful little boy, and a proud award-winning author. While this book was on pre-sale on Amazon, this book hit the number one spot on Amazon's romance writer's reference new release list, so I guess I'm also a best-selling author now too, LOL. I started my journey as a traditionally published author and later dived into self-publishing also. As a reader, I love romance, historical fiction, crime fiction, African-American, suspense and thrillers books. As a writer, I enjoy creating steamy stories with a diverse and multi-cultural line up within the romance, romantic suspense and general thriller and crime genres. When I'm not reading or writing my other passions include practising my French, fashion, drawing, make-up artistry,

spending time at my sewing machine dressmaking, watching make –
up and beauty tutorials on YouTube, letter writing and being a mum.

How Best to Use this Writing Reference Book and Prompts

Firstly, why even use writing prompts? Well, if my introduction
has not pushed you in the right direction to understand the benefits,
here's the real deal. We all get stuck! No matter how good of a
writer we are, how creative, or even how motivated, some days the
words or characters just run dry as hell. I've been there. So, to keep
it real, the purpose of this book is to help you avoid the dry spells as
much as possible and keep you fresh!

The best way to use this writing reference is to keep in mind these
five small things.

1. Make every prompt your own—you will find situations or
   people within each prompt. Nothing is set in stone, each
   prompt is just an idea or even outline or direction, if you
   like, for where you could head. I don't really recommend
   (unless you really feel drawn to my prompt) that you stick to
   it and not put your own spin on it somehow. Take a prompt
   and add, or subtract, what you feel suits your style,
   storytelling, experience or even desire. Basically, don't feel
   stuck with what you have; it's just an idea to get your juices
   flowing.
2. No matter your genre, steal it and use it! So, as you know by
   now, in the romance genre I'm a romantic suspense writer in
   principle. Yes, I have written other stuff and yes, I can write
   other stuff. But, I always default here because I love to read
   and write romantic suspense. So, with these prompts, I have
   kept them as generic as possible. This means if you like an
   idea, and wish to make it a paranormal, urban or fantasy
   romance, go for it! Like I said, don't feel stuck. Take the
   general idea and flip it to your own script.

3. Heat and steam levels are completely free for all! I like my romance steamy, maybe you're a sweet and clean writer, that's cool. Do what you wish in terms of heat levels, if you want to ramp up a prompt and make it high in heat...please do, I'd love to read it too!
4. Dip in and out of each month, week, etc. as you see fit, too. You can go through January-December or mix it up.
5. The last three months of the year, all the prompts are personal blogging prompts and I recommend that if you have not already, you really start to develop an author site or use your current one and do some personal blogging. (More on that later.) Again, you don't need to wait until October to start, start today!

Kim's Top Writing Tips—How to Write Great Romance!

Okay, don't panic I'm not about to tell you what or how to write. Personally, I hate that shit. I am myself and I have found my voice and I don't care who does not like it! You can't please all readers. I don't believe anyone should tell anyone how to write. However, I will share some things I have learned along the way, and to be honest I never realised I actually do this until reviewers would say 'well developed' 'realistic' 'good character development' 'great plot,' etc. So I will share my tips.

I've always been a big romance reader and have read some excellent, and some really bad romance. I read a few and it inspired me to write a blog post on my site 'How To Write Realistic Romance'. This was because I read a few and I found the plot, characters and people to cause so much doubt in my mind as a reader. I also feel that our genre as a whole has a reputation for being 'unrealistic' and full of 'fairy-tale romance.' I am sick of our genre being put down for bad stories that don't seem realistic, reasonable or even well-written. I believe we all have a role to play to get rid of this label our genre has. I don't claim to be an expert on 'the perfect well-written romance,' but I do claim to be a good romance writer.

How to Write Realistic Romance- Seven Tips

Everyone has their own style of storytelling. Believe me, I know! I'm a big rebel when it comes to writing in this genre! I don't believe in following the crowd; I hate it. I use the present tense and first person often. While a majority of this genre is third person and past tense. That said, I have been pulled to write this short 101 to help other aspiring romance writers, and anyone for that matter, as this simple advice can be applied across the board in all genres.

Characters

As a big reader, I love it when characters are so believable, realistic and engaging to read. When they're not, it can be a turn off. Not everyone is going to like your characters, and so what if they don't? They may be the wrong reader. The point is, when it comes to characters **who are they? This is my starting point before I think about my plot.** This is because, if you're going to write a realistic romance (or any genre story), the **characters will be what drives the plot.** Not and never the other way around. Remember this, think of your characters like this as the plot drivers.

Many writers may start with the plot and fill out characters. Cool, okay, if that's what's best for you. But you may find that you're so busy spinning your plot, your characters do unrealistic things and fall flat. I recently read two books—one romance and one other genre and this was my experience as a reader. If you know your characters well, you can portray them better. *They will react, think, move, talk, walk more vividly in your plot if you can focus on them first.* This helps massively with character development also.

Have you ever read a book and the characters are boring, or they are from a certain part of the world, or location yet they speak perfect English in their conversations? Hmmm, chances are the writer has skipped this part. Hence they speak perfect English, or just flat and not real. For example, when they are from the depths of south London for example and may have a different accent.

When I wrote a particular story for The Suspenseful Collection #2- Blurred Lines, I placed myself and Didi in the story lol. So when I portrayed myself in speech, I did not say, 'oh I'm so sorry about that, here let me help you.' I said, 'oh no, I'm sorry, 'er lemmie help ya'. That's because I'm from a certain part of London, and I would not, in casual conversation, speak like the Queen herself! Didi and I also had a Russian female in The Suspenseful Collection Volume #1 and of course she said, 'ello, yass 'ow can help you.' Rather than, 'Hello, yes how I can I help you.' The point is, little things like this matter, as well as who they are as people. You may think, yeah

Kim this is basic stuff. Trust me, you'd be surprised how many writers can easily forget, during character development.

This brings me to character development and thinking about it a little deeper. If you start by really thinking about who your characters are, outside of things like age, race etc., but who they are as people, where they have been, how they react to things and most importantly their flaws as people, you will have more rounded, believable and developed characters that drive your plot. Rather than a plot with flat characters, doing very unrealistic things.

Flaws and Growth

Okay so we all love a romance (or any genre book really) where the characters are not only real, but we as readers experience and see their growth. Don't forget this. Once you know who your characters are as people, *what flaws do they have?* And these flaws should *help drive the plot and show how they grow from it. Why?* Because it shows growth of each character, develops story and adds to reality! People have life experiences and we all grow from them, love and romance are no exception to the rule. If anything, love and romance really do allow us all to grow in some shape or form. So, give your characters a flaw or two, then make sure in the plot you show somehow that they have overcome it, or made steps to overcome it, and have changed or grown from it. This could be very subtle in your writing, it does not have to be over the top, but if you can show it, well, it should make good believable reading. It makes the characters real, the situations real, and the best bit is that it allows readers to experience the plot better.

Plot, Storyline and Storytelling

Okay, like I said, I've read a hella-lot of books, especially romance, and I feel a plot needs to be very realistic in as many books as possible, if not all. End of story, period and full stop!! This genre has such a reputation for delivering 'unrealistic stories' and I hate it,

12

and I will defend the genre I love to read and write until the cows come home! But, as a reader, I gotta say… yeah, there's some truth. Don't get caught up in trying to spin the perfect 'fairy tale' that things seem unreal. Ask yourself:

1. Would this really happen?
2. Could this even be possible?
3. And would my *characters* react like this, or how would they react and why?
4. What would my characters do in the situations I have placed them?

Where's the Challenges?

Now if you one, know your characters, and two, they have realistic flaws, they should not be doing unrealistic stuff, right? Good, glad we agree.

But, how do we keep it realistic? In my personal and humble opinion as a romance author, it's down to the challenges we give our characters. By this I mean, if there's no challenge and everything just fits into place this does not really make a great or even realistic story. We all know love and life does not roll like that, so it can come across as unrealistic. There needs to be some kind of 'challenge,' and I use the word loosely to mean some kind of 'debate', 'back and forth' 'questions' or even just a good 'ol dose of drama to keep the plot realistic. Don't go too mad (unless it's romantic suspense), but for good, clean, sweet romance a little challenge or dilemma, where a decision or choices need to be made, are key. And for romantic suspense, ha! Well, bring the heat with challenges! But keep them realistic to the characters, their environment and where they are at in life no matter what kind of romance you're writing. My best advice is, place your plot outline in the real world, in the time frame your story is set. So, if it's the present day would what you've outlined:

1. Have a chance of happening? Is this a realistic challenge to the character, time frame and who they are?
2. Could it be believable? What is a realistic challenge for this couple to either be together, come together, or hold them back for some reason? Where is the push and pull before they can be happy?
3. Does it go in line with the challenges, flaws, and issues you've given the characters and the overall plot? Does it work?
4. *Is there an actual challenge here worth telling? Is there more than sex in your plot? Does it develop into an actual story involving the characters?*

Pacing

All right now, I believe when or if there's an issue with pace, it might be because of one of two things. There's no story at all to tell, or secondly there is no story being told within the actual writing itself. And really pages are just being filled with words- *the story does not move!* The story does not have 'peaks' to keep the reader engaged. So, the pace seems like this ———————————————
———— all on one level and not really moving.

If you've really looked at your story line, plot, or the outline, whatever you choose to call it, you should be able to see if there is really a story, and eliminate point one. If so, where are the areas of *peak heat or tension* whatever you want to call it. Make them clear, for both you and the reader, then decide how you will build up to these peaks. By this I mean, what's your approach to bringing the readers to these peaks? Is it a sub-plot, surprise, mystery, a twist, or are you just ensuring that the story is told at a good pace and not dragged out?

You don't have to spin mystery, surprise, or suspense into a romance, it could just be a nice sweet story (something I'm not great at writing lol), or a contemporary romance. The point is, as you write your actual story keep up that damn pace! End as many chapters as you can with something interesting for the reader, and for the love of God keep moving. Without skimming or rushing, just make sure your pace is even. Here's very simple break down.

1. Start
2. Middle/climax
3. Level off/ OMG what will they do??/tension.
4. Bang…ending!

This is the simplest way I can put it with pace. I would *avoid leaving all the juicy stuff until the later part of your story.* Readers may fall off, lose interest or just feel that 'the pace is slow.' Keep them interested. As a side note, I mentioned reality as a big thing. So if you leave all the juicy stuff to the end, is this realistic to how life would go, in the situations you've placed your characters? Think about it. Do life and love just fit into place? Nope, I think not. Especially if you have a plot with some drama; if your characters just roll with it, is that really believable??? Adjust reaction, if you can, to fit the pace.

Insta-Love?

Lots of readers may dislike this in romance stories, I kinda do like it as a reader as long as it's believable. That's the deal breaker. If you like to write insta-romance, do your thang! I like to read it and have written it where characters connect fast. Remember what I said about pace… That said, if you serve up some insta-love *have you shown a reason 'why they can't get enough of each other and have fallen quickly?'* Give them some kind of connection. There is no use allowing your characters to say, 'I love you' (a lot), when you can't even see why they would love each other. It sucks, it's unrealistic and well, **more to the point,** where's the connection? How or why have they fallen for each other, even if it was pretty soon.

Now connection could be simple things: common interests, both want the same things in life, at the same point in life, etc. People connect when there is a connection no matter how small, we all know and have experienced this. Establish the connection….and keep it real! ***Show the reader why there is a believable chance these people would fall in love, even if is soon.*** I read a book recently and I could not see why the author's characters had a connection, and that placed doubt in my mind about the story, reality, and why these two people were in love. But they said 'I love you' a hella-lot though *rolls eyes.*

In my humble view, again, if they fall fast or not, show them falling, show the change of heart! Don't forget this, don't write a car crash of love and not show the change of heart, or the development of feelings in your story, even in a very subtle way as word count can be limited at times. If you do show this, it will help it to seem realistic. That's the name of the game.

How Much Sex is Too Much Sex?

Well, this is a hard balance to strike. But in my honest view as a reader yes, there is such thing as too much sex when and only when the rest of the plot is not developed enough. Simple. You decide on how much or little sex you want, it's not for anyone to say…***but just remember this cannot be the be all and end all of how you bring your story alive.*** Consider carefully where you place it, why and what it adds to your overall development of the actual story. Don't just scatter it around to fill pages and hope that a steamy story will hold your reader. It won't and probably can't when there is nothing else going on. *Shrugs shoulders* I'm just being honest as a reader, and that's my view as a writer too.

16

So off the top of my head these are a few approaches I take when writing romance. I wish every romance writer the best of luck! Let's fight that damn reputation we have for the genre, and pen some page-turning and realistic stories! *High five.*

Romance Tropes 101

Romance tropes are so helpful to us writers and readers. Think of them as a theme within your story, that drives it. Firstly, they allow you as the writer to know where you're going with your story. Secondly, readers know what they're in for and the kind of story they'll read. Here are the most popular romance tropes from what I have observed over the years of reading and writing within the genre. Sometimes authors I've read have mentioned what trope the story is within the book's blurb, so it's easy to see a theme too. Also, while you are writing you kind of notice it yourself what the theme is. For more details you can also check online on creditable writer's websites dedicated to writing romance for more details. I always suggest, when outlining your story, never and I mean never, forget the trope driving your plot. It will be a stronger story, I promise.

1. ***Friends to lovers-*** simply put, two characters who have a platonic relationship fall for each other.
2. ***Enemies to lovers-*** one of my favourites. Two characters who don't get on, or even like each other at first, come full circle and end up in love.
3. ***Second chances-*** beautiful romance! Also one of my favourites. Characters receive another shot at love. Whether they have had bad experiences with ex-partners, or they tried once before as a couple and it never worked out. This time it does.
4. ***Fake love, marriage or arrangement-*** two people get together purely for some other reason. Be it money or arranged by family or convenience. This is not a romance that initially starts with 'love' or even attraction, it's just what needs to happen for some other reason.

5. *'Wow, you've changed'*- characters are either together and one changes for the better or worse, or they have crossed paths before and now notice a change in them and some growth.
6. *Fated*- love that just seems like it's meant to be! Characters cross paths for a reason, in a situation, or place and there is a feeling of 'this is meant to be' soul mate connection.
7. *Inta love/ love at first sight (I prefer to call it 'insta connection' personally*)- characters meet and connect quickly! I do like this romance, but I recommend that you ensure that readers can understand and see why they have connected so quickly, a common ground or goal.
8. *Forbidden love*- for some reason two characters are not allowed or meant to be together. There is some conflict or stigma around this union that must be overcome if they are to move forward with it.
9. *Right person, wrong timing*- typically, two people who seem so perfect for each other connect, however the timing is wrong. There's a situation, person, or thing that's an obstacle to their union. However, they can reconnect later and cross paths again.

January

New Directions

January

It's the start of the year! Happy New Year writer, let's make it a great one. And even if it's not technically the new year as you read this but you're starting here, we're focusing on creating some great stories based on January's 'vibe.' In January, many of us consider it a 'new year, new start,' so here are some situations and people to ponder this month. Each involves some kind of 'new start or direction' for your hero and heroine. Remember you can switch genres and genders and make it your own.

1st January

Situation: Character A met character B at a New Year's Eve party last night. Thing is, character A was a little tipsy and can't remember much about them. It's New Year's Day, they're at home chilling working off their hangover, and character B calls. Write this scene: the first call, the conversation, and the lead up to their first date. How does the conversation and everything that leads up to the first date go? Keep in mind, character A can't remember much about character B, but they're single and free to mingle. If only they could remember who the person is. Create a love affair that starts off around this time of year (or any time), where at first character A can't remember their potential love interest, but they connect and end up having a HEA. The heat and steam levels are up to you!

Story Outline:

2nd January

People: Character A is sick and tired of the bullshit of last year; they're moving forward in a new direction. Write up a strong, fearless hero or heroine. What is it they're tired of? What are their goals? And what kind of man (or woman if that's the case) do they seek this year? Also, what are their conflicts that they are trying to overcome this new year? Tell their story, and why they are a little bit bitter about love. Then allow them to meet a potential new love interest via the new job they start this year. This new love has a heart of gold. Do they fall for it? Or do they resist this new direction of love because they are so jaded and cynical? As a challenge write them in the first person. Heat and steam levels are up to you.

Story Outline:

3rd January

People: A single father juggling work and family seeks love this year. You decide on why he's a single father. He's at the park with his kids when he meets a woman he's attracted to. What happens with these two? How do they cross paths and start talking? Do they meet again randomly? And who does he meet? Does this woman even like kids or willing to date a single father? You decide! The heat or steam level are up to you!

Story Outline:

January 4th

People: Today's date is World Braille Day, an international holiday celebrated in recognition of Louis Braille, the inventor of the braille language. Write a story about a person who is blind or partially sighted who finds love somehow. How does this happen? Where does it happen and who with? If you aim to make this a steamy story, don't forget to really bring out the emotions and use all the senses, as one sense (sight) is blocked for one character.

Story Outline:

January 5th

Situation: Character A broke off their engagement just before Christmas. They had cold feet. Now they regret it and are fighting for a second chance. Character B is conflicted over their head and heart; they are not sure if they should take them back. Write up an alpha male or female who will stop at nothing to get what they want from character B. Character B, on the other hand, has moved on in a new direction. You decide which. Character A fights to change this, so they now move in the same direction in life and love. You decide if there's a HEA or character B kicks them to the curb to continue in their new-found direction. Either way, give character B a HEA they deserve, and show growth in character A. Steam and heat levels are up to you, but make sure character A is strong, believable alpha type.

Story Outline:

6th January

Situation: Character A receives a surprise letter in the mail. It's not for them, it's meant for the previous tenant who moved out at Christmas. The letter is from a man (or woman) who would like to rekindle their love with the person who lived there before. Character A is looking for love too, and a new start this year. They ignore the letter, but one arrives every week! After a few weeks they decide to contact the sender. What happens to these two lonely hearts when they connect? Even if the sender was originally looking for someone they once connected with, allow them to experience some growth or change of heart as character A enters their life. The heat and steam level are up to you.

Story Outline:

7th January

People: Two people want to try something new, so it's time for a speed dating 'cute meet up.' It's a new year so they think 'what the hell.' Send two characters who would not normally be attracted to each other on a whirlwind of a love affair! They are not normally each other's type, but, being a new year and all they agree to one date after a speed dating event. How does it go? Show their conflicts and reservations and bring them full circle and in love! Opposites attract. Heat and steam level are up to you.

Story Outline:

8th January

Situation: Toward the end of last year, your characters kept bumping into each other on the journey to work or school etc. One of them summons the courage to approach the other as they return to work or school after the festive break. They meet on the train, bus, tram etc, some form of public transport. Give them both an interesting back story, one of them is new to the city or country. New love, new year! What happens? The heat and steam level are up to you.

Story Outline:

9th January

People: Your characters have not seen each other since they were teenagers. They were each other's first sexual experience. Suddenly, one of them has been offered a job at the same place as the other. That's not all. One of them is the other's line manager, boss or supervisor of some sort. One reports to the other. What happens between them? Take them both in a 'new direction' with love and life, considering the work situation and attraction from the past, and present. Create some push and pull, even danger, as they are now both employees of the same company and one is responsible for the other.

Story Outline:

10th January

Situation: Enemies to lovers, your characters dislike each other for whatever reason you choose. They have disliked each other from last year when they first crossed paths. Being a new year, they decide to put their differences aside. Write an 'enemies to lovers' story about these two. What happened between Christmas and New Year to allow them to break the ice in January? The heat and steam level are up to you.

Story Outline:

11th January

Situation: It's International Thank You Day today, and character A receives a random thank you card from character B. What did they do to help the other character out? Who are they to each other and how did they originally connect? Get creative with this. Was this a one-off connection or a favour that character B has never forgotten, and has always had character A in their thoughts? The sender turns into a potential love interest for character A from this connection, a simple 'thank you.' Move your characters in a new direction, just from this simple gesture of thanks. Heat and steam level are up to you.

Story Outline:

12th January

People: Off limits! That's todays theme. Write a story about a character who is fully aware their love interest is off limits. The interest could be their friend's sibling, a boss, co-worker whatever you want. Today's prompt is about love that develops when a person is off limits, and should really stay there. Change this direction and bring them towards each other. Give them conflicts and challenges that are external to their relationship, and internal for them as they try to fight their attraction. You decide if it's a long-lasting love affair or a one-time affair. Heat and steam level are up to you, but this could make a great steamy story! Love that's 'off limits' but somehow it moves in a new direction.

Story Outline:

13th January

People: A librarian and a plumber randomly meet after the librarian has a leak at home, then calls a workman/woman from the local phone directory to fix it. The librarian is a little shy and a total bookworm; you decide what the other character is like. It's Valentine's day in a month, so add this into your plot. What happens between these two people? Where are they in life romantically and emotionally, and what are their goals? Do they tie together, even if there is an attraction between them? How do they meet again and develop a romance? Heat and steam levels are up to you.

Story Outline:

14th January

People: Write a paranormal love story today. Cook up two characters that you would not normally create, and make this a paranormal love story. Witches, magic, and the unknown world! Go crazy. Give both of these character some kind of 'new direction' in their life, how do they come together from it?

Story Outline:

15th January

Situation: In Japan the second Monday in January is Coming of Age Day. It's a celebration that takes place for those who are reaching an 'age of maturity.' In this culture, the age of maturity is considered to be twenty years old. Write a story with a Japanese character aged about twenty years old, who falls for an older lover. The lover can be twice their age for example. What challenges do you think they would face? Your love interest can be from any culture or background, and you can set the story anywhere in the world, or even Japan. If you do this research well. Make this a 'forbidden love' story. What else could be holding them back, or causing doubt, other than age? Steam and heat level are up to you

Story Outline:

16th January

Situation: Dangerous love… let's write a story about how love can be dangerous for everyone involved. Why and how is this dangerous for character A and B. Make it suspenseful, the heat and steam level are up to you.

Story Outline:

17th January

Situation: Try your hand at an erotic story today! Your characters meet at a fancy dress party, and end up making a night of it. What happens at the fancy dress party and afterwards? Both characters never expected their one-night meet to go in the direction it is. Give them an unexpected new direction in love from this totally unexpected meeting at a fancy-dress party. Heat level…sky high!

Story Outline:

18th January

People: Try your hand at a historical fiction story today. Your romance trope is 'second chance love.' Character A and B both need a new direction and start with love. Why is this? What happened to their last lovers or even historically when it comes to love? Write a story that's based in a time period of the past that you are drawn to. The challenge is to keep in mind the era, social norms for men and women of that era, the language, style of love, dating and sex. Research if need be but your challenge is to keep this story as relevant and realistic as possible for this historical period. Give them both a new start together and second chance at love. Heat and steam levels are up to you.

Story Outline:

19th January

Situation: Today is Martin Luther King Day in the USA, (normally the third Monday in January), a national holiday to celebrate the work and life of the Civil Rights leader who fought to improve the quality of life for African-Americans. Write a story about love developing between characters of different backgrounds, who find it hard to connect due to stigma. Why is their love 'forbidden' or 'frowned upon,' or would have 'stigma' attached to it? Whatever you cook up for your characters give them the HEA they deserve after a fight for their love. One of them is not sure about the direction they are heading in love, due to the stigma. The other works hard to gain their love and move them in a new direction. Heat and steam level are up to you, so is the era you set the story. If you feel like spinning a paranormal, suspenseful, or erotic story go for it! Today's prompt is all about fighting for forbidden love in anyway your creative juices flow.

Story Outline:

20th January

People: Today is alpha male day. Write a story featuring a powerful businessman, what happens when his new secretary is just his type. The last secretary walked out on the job as he's a total ass most of the time, over the top and demanding. Write a story about love that crosses the line and pushes boundaries, between him and his new secretary. The secretary is no pushover. Craft a strong female who needs this job. She plans to stick it out even if he pushes her buttons. Your heroine somehow naturally changes your hero's direction and outlook on life, so he's softer and not such an ass once he crosses paths with her. Heat and steam level are up to you.

Story Outline:

21st January

People: Character A is a mature-in-years character, looking for a new start or direction with love. What are their fears? Experiences? Ups and downs? Set the story wherever you like in the world. Are they wealthy? Why have they not found love in their mature years? Or did they have a partner and they lost them? You decide! They meet a love interest that takes a fancy to *them,* and they are *younger*. Give these characters some push and pull but a HEA. Character A comes back around with their feelings and thoughts on character B. Heat and steam levels are up to you.

Story Outline:

22nd January

People: Write a story featuring a restaurant chef. He or she decides that they need a new direction this January, they start a job as a cruise ship chef so they can travel and do what they love, rather than be stuck in one location. They meet a love interest during their down time as the ship stops off in a country or location of your choice…what happens? Heat and steam level are up to you.

Story Outline:

23rd January

Situation: Character A is a taxi driver, character B is running late and flags down the taxi. This is a sweet little 'cute meet' for today's story. How does their love develop? Both characters are not really looking for love; you decide why this is. But it happens somehow after the cute meet in the taxi, sending them on a new direction. Heat and steam levels are up to you.

Story Outline:

24th January

Situation: Single mothers want love too! Write a story featuring a single mother who has moved away from her old city or town. The twist is that she finds romance in a very unexpected place. This unexpected place happens to be when she takes her child to the dentist or doctor. Her new love interest is the medial professional of your choice. How do they develop their love after the first appointment? The doctor or dentist has access to her contact details as her family health care provider, he takes the risk and contacts her what happens? He does not know for sure she's single but she had no wedding ring on... Heat and steam level are up to you!

Story Outline:

25th January

Situation: Love at first sight? It happens. Today let's write an 'instant connection' rather than 'insta love' story. Meaning your character's connection is quick, rather than the 'I love you' happening very quick with no connection. Two characters meet and there is chemistry right away, the reason for their connection is your choice, why can't they leave each other alone? The challenge is that character A is fighting it and feels it's too fast. Or is it? And why are they fighting it? Characters B won't take no for an answer, also their heartstrings are tugging. Is this a soul mate or 'fated' connection? Heat and steam levels are up to you.

Story Outline

26th January

Situation: 'Can I get that for you?' It all started when one person bought the other, their morning coffee. Write a story about two people who develop love, based on this meeting one morning. Send them in a new direction from the one they were going in, based on this cute meet.

Story Outline:

27th January

Situation: Bad timing, damn. Your characters are perfect for each other! Just a case of bad timing. Or something, or someone is standing in their way of being together. Why is it bad timing? What is the barrier? What other goals or situations do they have that cause the feeling of bad timing? You decide. Today let's write a story that has a lot of push and pull and emotional investment, but is now the right time 'with everything else' that's happening for one or if you like both characters? Give them a HEA that seems to work given the challenges you give them. Heat and steam levels are up to you.

Story Outline:

28th January

Situation: 'Baby, I want you back!' We've reached the end of the month and one character is reflecting and realises they made a 'mistake' with either their ex, or someone they briefly dated. They are on a mission to get back the love of their life, character B. What was the mistake character A made? And why are they now moving in a new direction towards character B? Heat and steam level are up to you.

Story Outline:

29th January

Place: It's pay day for many coming up. And also maybe a day to go out for drinks with friends, after a month of saving money post-Christmas. Write a story about two people that meet while out with a group of friends. Where are they? Who are they with? Did character A even really want to go out, do they feel happy they did as they bumped into character B? Heat and steam levels are up to you.

Story Outline:

30th January

Situation: Character A has a decision to make about their direction in life. What has brought them to this point? Give them two options or two possible directions they can head in, with their current life situation. Whatever direction they decide to take, allow this to be how they bump into or meet character B, who seems to be a very promising love interest. Send them both on an 'adventure.' Allow character A to take a risk of some sort with their direction that includes character B. Heat and steam levels are up to you.

Story Outline:

31st January

People: Let's try a possible romantic comedy today (or any kind of romance you feel drawn to). Character A is giving themselves thirty one days to find love, or at least someone to have some fun with. Why are they doing this? What do they do and who do they meet? How do they base their choices on who to take seriously? Make it fun, engaging and give them some kind of HEA or HFN. Heat and steam levels are up to you.

Story Outline:

February

Unexpected New Love

February

Ohhh the month of love. Valentine's Day is drawing near, the shops are decorated with chocolates and flowers, and love is in the air. This month, the focus is on the *development of love* after the new directions of January. This month, here are some situations and people related to the love that's developing, had developed and broke off, or about to develop after a 'cute meet' happens. As always swap the genres, genders and make things your own!

1st February

Situation: 'It's now or never.' Characters A and B have been dating for a while now and character A wants to take it to the next level. Their goal could be moving in together, marriage, kids etc you decide what the next level is. Character B is reluctant so they break up. Character A finds a new love and is about to get engaged. Oh no! Character B finds out. What happens with this love triangle? How does their old love affair develop again, after it broke off? Heat and steam levels are up to you.

Story Outline:

2nd February

Situation: 'Love from a distance.' It all started with a Valentine's Day card. Characters A and B work together or are friends; they have a friendly platonic connection of your choice in whatever context you decide. Character A has had their eye on character B for some time, they have fallen for them from a distance, but never let their true feelings be known. This year, character A decides to send character B a card to confess their feelings. How does character B respond? Is there anyone else involved for character B? You decide. Develop a love story that's formed on one side from a distance, allow character A to make a U-turn with their feelings of love. Heat and steam levels are up to you.

Story Outline:

3rd February

Situation: 'Sweep me off my feet.' Character A is planning to avoid all things love this February—they're single and suffering from a broken heart. Character A makes an unexpected connection with character B, who is also not really looking for love – so they say. They fall for each other! Give them a 'cute meet' and let the romance begin. Show their emotional change of heart and back and forth with their own internal feelings. 'I'm not looking for love, but damn I can't resist this person.' Etc. Your challenge is to show *emotional, character, and situation development* that's realistic and believable, from one state of mind and feeling to another state of mind or feeling. One of them sweeps the other off their feet this Valentine's, develop their love. Heat and steam levels are up to you.

Story Outline:

4th February

Situation: 'Rekindled love.' Your couple are going through a rough patch. You decide the challenges for them, give them internal and external factors that challenge them—keep them realistic to the couple. This Valentine's Day they have agreed to go to couples' therapy to work on their relationship and rekindle their love. What happens? What issues are they having? They make a promise to turn over a new leaf and attend therapy. Does it work? Develop their love from what once was in a rough state to a new direction. Give them a HEA. Heat and steam levels are up to you.

Story Outline:

5th February

People: 'Billionaire looking for romance.' Billionaire romances are so popular! Let's write a story about a billionaire who is seeking love this Valentine's Day. You can make him or her as wealthy as you want, but they earn their money in an honest way. However, they're fed up of being wanted purely for their wealth. They place an advert in a paper for love and poses as a less wealthy person. You decide how less wealthy they make themselves out to be, and what they do to hide their true wealth. They date a few people, then they meet a love interest. When it gets 'serious' how does the billionaire break the news to their love interest this Valentine's Day, that they are dating/in love with/or fallen for a billionaire? Develop the love between them. Heat and steam level are up to you.

Story Outline:

6th February

Situation: 'Lost and found love.' Characters A and B are looking for love, and character A has been stood up for a date. They stay at the restaurant or bar, drink themselves silly and end up leaving their wallet at the location. It's found by character B who was also at the same location. You creatively cook up character B, but they are single. Character A receives a call to let them know their wallet has been found, they meet character B to collect it, and unexpectedly cupid strikes. The challenge here is that character A wasn't stood up. Instead, something happened to their original date- what happened? Also, their original date wants a second chance. Character A decides to give the person who found their wallet a try, and not put all their eggs in one basket so to speak. What happens? Develop this new love connection and potential love triangle. Heat and steam levels are up to you.

Story Outline:

7th February

People: This Valentine's Day a professional matchmaker is looking for love. They are not one to mix business with pleasure and really enjoy their job, but they are lonely themselves. She/he finds love when one of her/his own clients, who they are matchmaking on behalf of, takes a fancy to them. This is a 'risky' situation for your matchmaker, with business and pleasure, but what happens? Develop their potential love connection. Heat and steam levels are up to you.

Story Outline:

8th February

Situation: Your female character has broken down in her car. Mr. Tall Dark And Handsome pulls over to give her a hand. The weather is terrible and she's far from her home with nowhere to stay; she is just passing through on her way to…you decide! Cupid strikes! Develop the love story for these two. Give them personal challenges of their own, but based on this meeting, is it fated? Do they help each other to heal in some way or provide what each other have been looking for? You decide how this develops. Heat and steam levels are up to you.

Story Outline:

9th February

Situation: A case of mistaken identity. Character A thinks they already know character B from their past. There was some kind of 'conflict' with character B, but it's the wrong person. The mistaken person character B, does however feel attracted to character A. Can character A overcome the shock of the similarity with the person they have mistaken character B for, and get to know them? Develop the love between these two. What happens? What challenges do they have? Heat and steam levels are up to you.

Story Outline:

10th February

Situation: Character A has some kind of accident on the street; you decide how serious, life threatening etc. A passer-by is a medical professional who happens to be in the right place at the right time. Why are they there? The medical professional—Character B, offers their help and remains in contact with character A. They help them to recover, and cupid strikes. Develop this storyline between them. Heat and steam levels are up to you.

Story Outline:

11th February

People: Character A has a very poor sense of direction; they end up lost and randomly bump into character B. Where is the character A going? Why are they in that location? What are they looking for? How does character B know how to help character A find all that they are looking for? This is a 'cute meet' between strangers, then love develops following the meeting. Heat and steam levels are up to you.

Story Outline:

12th February

People: Today is Darwin Day, a day celebrated around the world to reflect and celebrate the work Charles Darwin did. Write a story featuring a science geek as your main character. Make this a 'cute meet' between character A—the scientist, and character B, with a touch of unexpected love for our science geek! They could be shy and unsure of themselves, but highly intelligent. However, once they cross paths with character B, character B brings out a new side to them. Develop this love between one highly intelligent person, who does not have the best social skills maybe, and someone who they think would not normally look twice at them. Heat and steam levels are up to you, but this could make a nice steamy story!

Story Outline:

13th February

People: Character A is new to the area; they just moved there. Why are they here? What have they left behind? And why have they left it? They have a very sexy neighbour—character B, who they see from their balcony across the way. Character B invites them over for dinner to get to know them, or they connect somehow as they live in the same location. What happens between these two when Valentine's Day approaches? And following their first casual dinner? Heat and steam levels are up to you.

Story Outline:

14th February

Situation: It's my birthday today! Yes me, Kim. So let's write a story featuring characters that 'cute meet' at some kind of party or celebration. Both character A and B are here. Why are they at this celebration, whose birthday or celebrational event is it? Why do they both find themselves there? Character A dragged their feet all the way there, they never really wanted to go. Develop their love story after they meet at the party or celebration. What do they have in common why they are both at the party? Heat and steam levels are up to you.

Story Outline:

15th February

People: Post Valentine's Day come down, let's write an 'anti V-Day' story. Characters A and B had a terrible Valentine's Day this year. But somehow become connected a couple days or weeks later. How do they cross paths? Why was Valentine's Day so bad for them? What do they have in common with their experience of Valentine's Day this year? Once they connect, develop their love moving forward. Heat and steam levels are up to you.

Story Outline:

16th February

People: 'Runaway bride' is today's theme. Write a story featuring a woman who didn't want to marry the man she said yes to. Why did she change her mind? Why did she leave him in the end? How did she leave him? Now single and her ex-husband-to-be is in the past, she has fallen into the arms of a new man. How did this happen for her? Develop the love story between the runaway bride and her new love interest. Give both conflicts and show the emotional growth to a HEA. Heat and steam levels are up to you.

Story Outline:

17th February

Place: Cupid strikes between two dog walkers. Where did they meet with their dogs? And how does their love develop? Heat and steam levels are up to you.

Story Outline:

18th February

Place: Cupid strikes in an office; let's write an 'office drama.' Characters A and B work side by side in a work setting, in any profession or context you choose. Develop their love, and the push and pull between mixing work and pleasure. Do they like each other? Or secretly desire each other? Do they get caught? You decide. Heat and steam level are up to you.

Story Outline:

19th February

Situation: Start your story off with "the first time I saw them I just knew." What did your character know? Was it a negative or positive knowing they had? How did this love affair start and develop? And what conflicts or challenges take place? Heat and steam levels are up to you, place this story in any genre you feel drawn to.

Story Outline:

20th February

Situation: Start your story off with, "I feel so different when they are around me." What is your character feeling, and why? Make this any genre you want. Heat and steam level are up to you.

Story Outline:

21st February

Situation: It's International Mother Language Day, celebrated around the world to acknowledge diversity and culture. Today let's write an interracial romance, and if you already write this genre of romance, good for you! Today, let's create a story with characters from opposite backgrounds that are **not sure about dating outside their race**, yet **they wish to as they are curious about it.** Write this from each character's POV. What challenges do you think each character will have given their own background? Give them a 'cute meet' of your choice; the aim is to create a multicultural romance that shows good character, emotional, and love development from both POVs. The whole story should have a full line-up of characters from races or places that you never normally use or have featured in your work before. Heat and steam levels are up to you.

Story Outline:

22nd February

People: Today try your hand at writing a 'dark and paranormal romance.' Your female or male vampire has come across a human they like the look of, but they don't want to feed on them. Your human character somehow got themselves involved in the dark world of the immortal, how? Your vampire character is cold, mean, and does not miss being human at all, but now they strangely want companionship from this human. Is it possible for this human to stir up 'unnatural' feelings of love within this vampire? What happened for this cold vampire to feel this way? Develop a love story between the human and vampire. Keep it steamy if you wish.

Story Outline:

23rd February

Situation: Let's write another paranormal story today. Character A lost their lover some time ago. They have not moved forward in a new relationship. Their ex makes contact from beyond the grave, do they believe it's them? How do they react? It turns out that the contact is to warn character A not to get involved with a particular new person they cross paths with. What is the reason they are warning them? What 'dark secret' or surprise does this new person— character B have, that character A needs to be aware of? Develop a love story for character A with character B who's potentially no good and involves paranormal activity from their ex. Heat, steam and creepiness levels are up to you.

Story Outline:

24th February

People: Write a story about love that develops between two people suffering some kind of loss. Characters A and B both have this to overcome; you decide what the loss is. How do they help each other move forward? How do they meet? And how does the love form and develop? Give them realistic and heart felt challenges. Heat and steam levels are up to you.

Story Outline:

25th February

People: 'I can't stand your ass!' Characters A and B are falling in love but can't have each other for some reason. Place a barrier in their way that causes them to dislike each other, but not another person—be more original and get creative. This could be anything you wish other than another person. This is 'love that's unattainable because of x, y, z.' However, they overcome it and it develops. Heat and steam level are up to you.

Story Outline:

26th February

Situation: Write a story starting, "Every time he/she looked at me." What happened to character A? Was it good or bad? How did the look help to develop love? Heat and steam level are up to you.

Story Outline:

27th February

People: Two failed artists cross paths somehow. Characters A and B are suffering some kind of personal loss, be it love, money, or something else. Create a bitter-sweet love story about love or a life situation that came crashing down for each character, and then, somehow they find love in the most unusual place and circumstances. Think outside of the box. How do these two characters connect through their past pain, or current situation in life and love of the arts? Heat and steam levels are up to you.

Story Outline

28th February

Situation: Today is romantic suspense day! Character A has something to hide. They move away and find a new job and a new way of life, as well as a new personal identity via a name change. In this new location, they rebuild themselves but are constantly wondering if their secret will remain a secret. They connect with a love interest—character B, but the person they connect with is somehow linked to their past. Character A finds out when they are in too deep with character B. What happened in the past? What is character A running from? And do they successfully keep their secret? How does this love develop with things in the shadows? Set this story in any location you want but keep it suspenseful. Heat level… ummm? Let's go with sky high!

Story Outline:

29th February

Situation: It's a leap year at the time of writing this, so today let's write a story with a role reversal. Your female character is set to propose marriage to her love interest. She is very nervous about this, but the reason she would like to propose is because she almost lost her love interest. You decide the 'situation' where she almost lost her lover, be it via a life or death situation, break up, or something else creative. Switch the roles—your female MC is set to pop the question to character B. Does he accept? Is there push and pull? Give them a HEA since there was a 'situation' that almost caused them to lose each other. Heat and steam levels are up to you.

Story Outline:

March

Fresh Starts and New Beginnings

Welcome to March, writers. In many parts of the world it's the start of spring time. This month, here are some prompts that focus on that 'fresh new feeling' between your characters. As always, switch genres, genders, locations to your own creative flow, and vary your heat levels.

1st March

Situation: 'Love found online.' Character A has been searching for love online for some time now. They've had no luck, then they stumble across character B. It's a 'refreshing' change from the experiences they have had online with previous people. Character A's conflict is whether they can trust this new fresh feeling, even if it feels fantastic and is what they are looking for. What experiences did your character have before? Why is this new connection different or difficult even if they like it deep down? Do they take the risk and it pays off with a lasting love this time around? How does character B react to character A's coolness? Create a story with some emotional push and pull about love found online. Maybe they're in different parts of the world? Who knows?— you decide. Steam and heat levels are up to you.

Story Outline:

2nd March

People: Character A is from a small town, and they move to a large city away from friends and family. Why did they do this? When they moved, they loved the fresh feeling of the city, new pace of life, and how it compares to a small town, but they've become lonely and started hoping, wishing and searching for love. What happens when a 'small town' character experiences the city life, and all it has to offer with character B— a potential love? Heat and steam levels are up to you. Give them conflict and challenges too.

Story Outline:

3rd March

People: Today, let's try and write a western story! Have it feature a hot cowboy and an adorable heroine who both need a 'fresh start.' I wonder if you have ever tried this genre? Today's the day, writer. What do you know about this genre? Research it and put your own spin on it with a touch of romance. Heat and steam levels are up to you.

Story Outline:

4th March

Situation: Characters A and B lost contact some time ago, how did this happen? They *did* get close and character A up and left without any explanation. Why did they leave? Character B was left heartbroken, but managed to pull their life back together. Their paths cross as one of them moves to the same town as the other after all these years. Character A has some explaining to do and has been filled with guilt for a while. What happens when these two people finally come face to face? And is the past forgotten? Create a fresh new feeling and direction after some conflicts between them. Show great character growth too. Heat and steam levels are up to you.

Story Outline:

5th March

Situation: Characters A and B ultimately want the same thing. It could be a job, or another person, or even to win something. How do they end up falling for each other, when they start out as on opposite sides? Create a fresh new feeling once they realise what they really want is not this 'thing' but each other. Heat and steam levels are up to you.

Story Outline:

6th March

Situation: Characters A and B are married, but for different reasons other than love. What was the reason, why did they need to get married? Is everything going well? Explore how these characters you place in this union, for reasons other than love, grow to actually love each other. They can have a HEA or HFN. Heat and steam levels are up to you.

Story Outline:

7th March

Person: Character A has not had much luck with searching for love, or with the people that they have dated. They seek out or cross paths with a modern witch or some form of magical worker (character B) who helps them find love, and bring something fresh to their love life. Character B casts a spell for character A; how does it go? This could even be a romantic comedy, suspense, paranormal any sub-genre you wish! Heat and steam levels are up to you.

Story Origin:

8th March

People: It's International Women's Day today! Create a strong, fearless female based on or using parts of whatever the theme is for this year's International Women's Day. Do a Google search and find out what is happening this year. If the theme does not grab you, then your second prompt is to create a story featuring a very strong, sassy, and bossy Queen who will stop at nothing to get what she wants. What does she want in life? How does she meet character B? Character B is her match both in and out of the bedroom. What happens when they collide? Heat and steam levels are up to you.

Story Outline:

9th March

People: Character A is infatuated with someone they have their eye on, and they start to do very weird, strange and dangerous things to gain their attention and closeness. Character A does not have to be mentally unwell or less stable (unless you want them to be and feel comfortable writing this), however, it's their strength of attraction or desire for character B that drives their actions. How did they come across character B, how does their infatuation start, how does this trigger dangerous or strange actions? How does the other— character, B, react? Where does this lead to? Heat and steam levels are up to you.

Story Outline:

10th March

Situation: Imagine two lovers in a happy relationship who suddenly find themselves in some form of danger, or tricky situation together. The situation has come about due to a connection, past event, or action of one of these characters. What happens with their love affair as it takes on a 'new situation' or feeling? Create some suspense with the element of danger that they face. Heat, steam and suspense levels are up to you!

Story Outline:

11th March

People: Character A has left their career behind and decided to go travelling. Why have they done this? They head to a hot, exotic, and beautiful location as a backpacker, for a new fresh outlook on life. Who do they meet there? They find a new love interest, and then need to decide whether they should stay or continue travelling. What happens in this love affair? Take character A in a fresh new direction compared to the ideas they had, just before they set off travelling.

Story Outline:

12th March

Situation: Character A falls for their child's nanny/babysitter. How does this happen? Your character can be a single parent if you want. You decide if the other parent passed away or something else happened. However, this is a 'new feeling' of desire that happens between the parent and babysitter/nanny, ***no prompt towards infidelity*** as a central part of the plot is being advocated here, this is romance after all! This could be a real sweet story. Heat and steam levels are up to you.

Story Outline:

13th March

Situation: Spring is well and truly in the air by mid-March in many parts of the world. Give characters A and B a 'fresh new love experience' different from the past, one they have been waiting for patiently. Write a heart-felt 'second chance love', or 'fated' story that's set in the *springtime* or has spring as an important part to the story. Character A and B's 'cute meet' happens while they are both out enjoying an early morning walk or run, or they are in some way making the most of the start of this season. What pulls them to each other? How does their connection bloom into love? Bring all the emotions, all the feels and heart-felt scenes and cook up a true love story in the springtime.

Story Outline:

14th March

Situation: Characters A and B are in a relationship and they need to spice up their connection. They are both complacent, bored, busy with work and kids (if they have any), but not considering seeing other people or leaving. They just need to rediscover each other and rekindle their love in a fresh way. They could be married or not, but they have been together for some time and past the 'honeymoon stage.' Character A has a very deep, dark, or even kinky fetish. They share it with their partner, and what happens when they do? What happens with this couple's relationship as they venture into new fetishes or things they have never done? You decide on how kinky or quirky the fetishes are. Breathe new life into their relationship with this new kink or fetish, send them in a new direction. Heat and steam levels down to you.

Story Outline:

15th March

People: Two close friends decide to take their relationship to the next level. What pushed them to do this—was there an accidental kiss? A drunken confession of feelings? Or did one of them up and leave their ex, then fall into the arms of their friend? You decide. It's a 'fresh new feeling.' Both see each other differently, what happens? Does it work? There will be challenges as they enter this new direction and feeling toward each other, what are they? Create a 'friends to lovers' story. Heat and steam levels are up to you.

Story Outline:

16th March

Situation: Characters A and B broke up due to one of them not pulling their weight. You decide what the 'weight' is. They went their own separate ways finally, and they have missed each other, but one feels that the other ultimately won't change. They meet again, when a mutual friend invites them to a wedding somewhere outside of where these characters live. They meet up at the location and some time has passed since the break-up. Is there still a connection? What happens? Give them a 'fresh start' after some push and pull. Maybe even some added drama to the wedding party! Heat and steam levels are up to you.

Story Outline:

March 17th

People: Give 'Cinderella' a modern and fresh take. Your heroine always feels like the 'ugly sister.' Her friends, siblings, co-workers, etc outshine her, according to her. How does this change when she meets Prince Charming? What does she experience before hand to make her feel like the 'ugly sister' in life? Where does she meet her Prince Charming, in what situation or setting? How does this change her? Develop a fairy-tale ending for your heroine, in a modern and fresh way. Heat level, suspense, and even the era the story is set are up to you. Get creative with your approach to Cinderella's traditional fairy-tale story.

Story Outline:

18th March

People: Give the theme 'beauty and the beast' a modern and fresh take. One of your characters is far from a 'beauty' in the traditional sense, however they manage to find love regardless of their shortcomings. Think outside of the box for a character who is not 'handsome' or 'pretty' or 'sexy.' Give your character a real physical flaw—this could have happened via an accident, birth, etc. How did they get this flaw? How did the flaw change them? What was, or is, their experience of living with this flaw? How do they go about finding love again? How, why, and where does character B fall for your flawed character A? Heat and steam levels are up to you.

Story Outline:

19th March

People: Create a 'rags to riches story' with some romance. Get creative, that's all I'm giving you! You decide the genre, genders, locations and heat levels.

Story Outline:

20th March

Situation: What genre have you always wanted to try, but never had the guts to? Or doubted your ability to write a romance story in the genre, era, location etc? Today the 'fresh new start' is for you, the writer. Pick a genre that you've never dabbled in much, then create characters A and B. A is 'trying to survive in this world.' Character B is of a similar age and a little unsure of themselves, due to something. You decide what 'something' is and what 'trying to survive' means for each character. How and where do they meet, with these motivations and goals they have? Give them a reason or situation that draws them to each other, and their love for themselves as well as each other is fresh and new. Heat and steam levels are up to you.

Story Outline:

21st March

People: It's World Down Syndrome Day. Character A has this, or cares for someone with this, or falls for someone who has this disorder. For this prompt bring your imagination alive and get creative. Here's your chance to research this disability and create a heart-felt love story. Bring out all the 'feels' readers love such as love, loss, growth and conflicts. Heat and steam levels are up to you.

Story Outline:

22nd March

Situation: It's World Water Day, celebrated around the world to highlight the need to conserve fresh water in countries and places that need it. Today's prompt is based around water. Character A has a near death experience by the water, and was saved by character B. The person that saved them is just who they need in their life, however when they wake up in hospital they can't remember who character B is, or why they were by the water. What happened to them by the water? Why were they there? How do these two connect moving forward? Give character A a fresh take on life and love after nearly losing their life, and being saved by a potential love interest— character B. Heat and steam levels are up to you.

Story Outline:

23rd March

Situation: Today is World Meteorological Day, celebrated around the world to raise awareness about the environment, weather and climate. Character A is weather reporter and journalist for a local TV station. A new member of their camera crew—character B takes a fancy to them. Character B notices character A while filming on the job. Send these two on a whirlwind of a love affair! Does Character A respond to character B or do they blow hot and cold like the weather? Give these two a fresh new experience with love that they have not experienced before! Heat and steam levels are up to you.

Story Outline:

24th March

People: It's World TB (tuberculous) day today. While this is a terrible and very infectious disease, it's today's prompt too. And you have two, today is also the eight-fourth day of the year and as I wrote this two ideas came to me!

1. Your character is a medical professional or some kind of medical researcher who takes a job abroad, to either Africa or south Asia where the highest cases of TB are found. They head away to find a 'fresh start' after a 'bad timing' situation, with their last partner. That said, they remain amicable as friends. What happens when they tell their ex-partner they are going halfway around the world? If they go, what happens when they reach their new destination?

2. Character A is a medical secretary, and they only dates for eight-four days. After a lot of short-lived relationships, they no longer want to emotionally invest only to end up the loser, as their dates lose interest or don't want to commit, etc. This is until character B gives them a new outlook and fresh start. Character A is torn between moving past the eight-four day mark, or breaking it off. Who is character B? Develop the love story between them? Heat and steam levels are up to you.

Story Outline

Story Outline #2

25th March

Situation: Character A has an opportunity of a lifetime. Somehow, life has presented them with the chance to work abroad and a fresh new experience via work. (Depending on the age you wish them to be, you decide what they will do work-wise). Once there they have a 'buddy' to help them settle in with their new job and life, who also works for the same company in that country—character B. However, character B really dislikes them from the get-go. They either wanted the job character A has, or they generally dislike them as they are foreign. Turn this into an 'enemies to lovers' story with a HEA that's abroad, with a 'fresh outlook' for each of them as people. Their POV changes. Conflict, drama, push and pull, and how do they put aside their differences – you decide. Heat and steam levels are up to you. Pick a lovely setting! Allow your readers to escape.

Story Outline:

26th March

People: Give a widow or widower (character A) a fresh start with love. They can have grown up children who have left home, or is currently raising younger children now, you decide. Character B is their love interest, who is it—someone new or someone from their past? You decide. Here's the challenge: if it's someone from their past, there's some kind of 'dark or suspenseful' history between these two characters, can they overcome the past and fall in love this time around? Heat and steam levels are up to you.

Story Outline:

27th March

Place: Characters A and B are two old friends or ex-lovers who now live in totally different locations, be it countries or cities. Create a life for them either as single or in a bad relationship etc. Character A tracks down character B as there's an 'emergency or tragic event' that's connected to them both. This pulls them both back to the *place and location* they met originally to manage this drama. In order to get through this 'tragic event or state of emergency' you create for them, they support each other as friends but this grows and a 'fresh start' love happens. Keep it suspenseful if you wish, heat and steam levels are up to you. This could even have a hint of mystery, or paranormal with the *place* they are pulled back to. Get creative with this one—there's so much you can do!

Story Outline:

28th March

Situation: Today is Earth Hour Day. It's celebrated on the last Saturday of March each year, in order to remind us to be mindful of energy consumption and the environment. So today let's craft a story where a loss of energy or power connects two lonely hearts. Characters A and B live in a location that's a little remote, or they are staying there for a reason of your choice—think small town or countryside. When there's a loss of power they are thrown together, character A knocks on the door of character B for help. Possibly they need candles or something, you decide. They get a surprise when it's someone new that has moved in. What happens between these two once they cross paths during the loss of power? Heat and steam levels are up to you. This could be a 'fated love' trope. Also, who are these characters, what's happening in their individual lives right now?

Story Outline:

29th March

People: Character A is completely disillusioned with the idea of love. They are sick of it, bitter, won't entertain it, and can think of better ways to spend their time than dating and falling in love. They have struck it off their bucket list for good! Even sex is off limits— they can't bring themselves to have meaningless sex anymore. They haven't had any sexual contact with another person for over a year. What happened in their past to make them feel this way? Who or what are they blaming for the way they feel? This can be a very deep reason, think outside the box of an 'ex-lover who broke their heart' and get creative. This changes when they meet that one special person, and that's character B. However, your character that is disillusioned will not give them an easy ride. Chase, thrill and back-and-forth is what happens; it's a feeling of 'catch me if you can.' Allow their love interest, character B, to finally catch them and give this disillusioned poor soul a new life, love and outlook after the thrill of the chase. Heat and steam levels are up to you.

Story Outline:

30th March

People: Character A is a total player, dates multiple people, including having sex with them, and really has no regard for anything but their own satisfaction. Character B is a serious, loving, and tender-hearted person who really would love to settle down. What happens when these two personalities collide? Where and how do they meet? Give them both a fresh outlook and HEA that readers would not expect. Heat and steam levels are up to you.

Story Outline:

31st March

Situation: Character A has agreed to a friends-with-benefits arrangement with character B. How and why did this happen? Things seem to be going well, they have had some fun dates. Character A notices that character B is distancing themselves and at the same time wonders about a future with them. They find out that character B is now seeking something more serious, but they didn't consider character A due to their agreement—there's someone else in the picture! However does this situation work out? Heat and steam levels are up to you.

Story Outline:

April

Love in Unusual Places

Welcome to April. There's a saying about this month: 'April showers' and 'April showers bring May flowers' some may have heard. Where I'm from, this is very true, you never know when it may suddenly start raining unexpectedly. This month it's all about the unexpected when it comes to love. As always, change genres, genders and heat or steam levels.

1st April

Situation: It's April Fool's Day! Today, try your hand at a romantic comedy or rom-com. What happens when characters A and B meet, in any setting you wish, and something funny happens that connects them? How does their connection follow on after this funny event? Heat and steam levels are up to you, but keep it humorous and laugh out loud funny!

Story Outline:

2nd April

People: Today is International Children's Book Day. Your main character is an aspiring children's author who meets an English teacher at a bookshop. What happens when they meet? Character A has gravitated to this profession as they long for children of their own. Create a feeling of something unexpected about one of them, or an unexpected event in their romance. Heat and steam levels are up to you.

Story Outline:

3rd April

People: A fashion model and a police officer meet in an unexpected way. The officer wants to arrest the model for something. Later, love blooms when they cross paths again. How do they meet, and what was the reason for arrest? Heat and steam levels are up to you.

Story Outline:

4th April

People: A detective crosses paths with character B, the detective wants to get to know them. The problem is that they're not sure if character B is 'really that into them.' When they start dating and getting to know one another, character B seems to be holding back. What are they hiding? As they date and love develops an unexpected situation arises around character B's shadiness. Being a detective, character A has to dig deep. What is it they find out? Can character A trust character B and remain in love with them? How does this love affair end up once the cat is out the bag? Heat and steam levels are up to you.

Story Outline:

5th April

Situation: This month's prompts are all about the unexpected, and you expect me to give you all the ideas! Here's something unexpected—think of something that happened to you in a relationship that was unexpected. Now, turn this situation or part of it into a fiction story with a HEA. Remove yourself from the situation and create characters and put **THEM** in the situation that happened to you. Heat and steam levels are up to you.

Story Outline:

6th April

Situation: Today is World Health Day, founded by the World Health Organisation (WHO). Today, your character has currently or has developed (you decide) an illness. It could be terminal or not as serious. Whatever the health issue is for them they need to find and hire a carer. Your character and carer form a tight bond. It does turn into more than friendship, which is unexpected, but do they tell each other? And if/when they do, how does this pan out for them? Is there a HEA or does this end as a soul mate connection, but a bitter-sweet ending and the ill character passes away? You decide. Heat and steam levels are up to you?

Story Outline:

7th April

People: Characters A and B have been dating for a while. Their anniversary is coming up and they've planned celebrations for it. Character A receives a call, letter, or contact with some unexpected news. This could be life-changing, shocking, good, bad, or places some strain on the union. You decide, but make sure it impacts on this couple's union and celebration. When character A receives the news, what's their next move, and how does the other character react? Give them some challenges, some push and pull, and bring them on a U-turn back to happiness in a twisty romance that ends up with them back in love and a HEA. Heat and steam levels are up to you.

Story Outline:

8th April

Situation: Character A is left an unexpected amount of money in a distant relative's will. That distant relative's non-blood-related stepchild is the executor of their will— character B. They get in contact with character A to let them know of their new fortune. As they both battle with the grief of the loss of the person they held close for different reasons, unexpected feelings develop. What happens, do they move forward? Or is this 'forbidden love' due to the connection? Allow the characters to fall in love with each other, using the support they provide each other and get creative. Heat and steam levels are up to you.

Story Outline:

9th April

People: Character A is wealthy, character B is not as wealthy. Character A has a great-paying job, background and education etc, and character B doesn't. They meet in an unexpected situation or place you place them, and feelings develop unexpectedly after casual dates and a friends-with-benefits situation. Does character A dare to cross the line once feelings develop on both sides? And with a person who does not fully live up to their expectation financially, or due to their background? Give them some challenges to overcome and grow in order to make this a lasting love. Heat and steam levels are up to you.

Story Outline:

10th April

Situation: Characters A and B meet, date and fall in love. Their relationship is going really well, and it gets to a point where marriage is even considered. They are really happy until character A has a life-changing situation happen. It could be a loss of a job, illness, the death of someone close, or whatever you decide. This life-changing situation places strain on them and their happy love and future plans. Does character B stay with them and remain committed? This unexpected change brings a new direction for character A and for this union. Following this, bring them on a U-turn so they're back to a happy place or a HFN. Heat and steam levels are up to you.

Story Outline:

11th April

Situation: Let's try a historical fiction today. Your characters are a young family or couple living in any part of the world you wish. Unexpectedly, your male character is called away to serve in the army. How does this young family and romance survive? Are there children involved? And does he return home or does something tragic happen while he is in service and she finds new love? You decide on the direction, there are many possibilities! Heat and steam levels are up to you.

Story Outline:

12th April

People: Characters A and B are both some kind of law enforcement officers—detectives, police officers, etc. They are partners who work together. Character A has a strong attraction to character B. One evening while out on duty together, character A tries to kiss character B unexpectedly; they have had a burning passion for them for some time. What happens between these two? Do they cross the line? How does their work relationship end up as lovers? Does anyone find out? Unexpectedly, the female character becomes pregnant. Are they both happy? Heat and steam levels are up to you.

Story Outline:

13th April

People: It's romantic suspense today! Character A is a mafia boss, drug lord, or some form of 'bad-boy.' He has a number of the local law enforcement offers on his payroll in order to keep them in line, and the law away from his activities. Character B, the new female boss, steps in. She now oversees the police department for the area he operates in. Somehow her path crosses with the mafia boss, and they start to play a dangerous game when she starts doing her best to bring him and his organised crime ring down. This leads to them somehow unexpectedly fall into bed with each other, then catch feelings for each other. What happens in this situation, with these people with opposing goals in life and work who click romantically? Does she bring him down and clean up the area he operates in? Or does he overpower her with his love and desire? You decide. Heat, steam and suspense levels are down to you.

Story Outline:

14th April

People: Characters A and B are backpackers or globe hoppers who take off on an adventure separately. Give them their own individual reasons why they do this. Their paths cross in a location they randomly decide to travel to next. They experience lots of romance, adventures and new experiences that draw them close. What happens with this unexpected connection between them, in this great location? Heat and steam levels are up to you.

Story Outline:

15th April

Situation: Write a story about two people who cross paths when there's a sudden downpour of rain or bad weather. Character A has an umbrella for shelter, character B doesn't. Send them on a 'cute meet' love affair. They both were not really looking for love, but this connection happens unexpectedly, from a simple gesture of kindness with shelter from the 'April showers.' Heat and steam levels are up to you.

Story Outline:

16th April

People: Let's write a romantic comedy, or rom-com. Your female character is obsessed with horoscopes and star sign compatibility. What happens when she unexpectedly meets character B, who is her usual type visually, but his star sign is one of her least favourite, or the same as one of her ex-partner's that broke her heart. Heat and steam levels are up to you.

Story Outline:

17th April

People: Let's try a young adult genre story. Characters A and B are both college students. Character A is new to the town or city and does not have any friends here. They are a little geeky and keep themselves to themselves most of the time. Generally they are more reserved in nature. They accept an invite to go away on a weekend camping trip. It's an unexpected invite and they debate whether to go, but in the end they do. Here they cross paths with character B, who is Mr. or Ms. Popular, who turns out to be their first real unexpected experience of romance. What happens to character A, who is normally shy and reserved, and this new unexpected connection? Heat and steam levels are up to you, but this is a young adult story—keep that in mind.

Story Outline:

18th April

People: Create a fantasy world where characters are not fully human, there are two clans in opposition, and there is a war over territory or a sacred place. Both sides of the population are ruled by an alpha male figure, with a strong clan of their own kind behind them. These rulers despise each other, but one ruler is taken down unexpectedly and the new ruler is a female who steps up in his place to rule over that clan. She also happens to be the mother of a secret 'love child' *for the opposing clan ruler*. They have a past, and no one knows about it; it was kept a secret. What happens when she steps up to rule over her clan that is in opposition with the other clan, and it's alpha male leader who is her child's father? Heat and steam levels are up to you.

Story Outline:

19th April

People: Character A is escaping an abusive relationship with a young child. They move away to a very different location where they both face a hard time settling into a new way of life. You decide on the challenges. Character B offers a helping hand, and also unexpected love. What happens between these two? What are both of their challenges? Heat and steam levels are up to you. This could be a fantastic heart-warming story there's so much you can do, get creative and dig deep.

Story Outline:

20th April

Situation: Characters A and B broke up years ago, and it was a bitter one. They haven't been successful with finding 'the one' as yet. They meet via a new online dating website where profiles are pictureless, but users complete a detailed matchmaker questionnaire on their views on love and marriage, in order to allow people to really get to know each other properly and not just at face value. They meet on the first blind date after getting to know each other via the website. What happens when they unexpectedly come face to face all these years later, and experience the surprise of realising that, the profile of the pictureless person they clicked with is someone they already had a bitter break up with? Heat and steam levels are up to you.

Story Outline:

21st April

People: Character A has just moved into a new home. They find a handful of thick journals in the attic. They start to read them and learn about the person who wrote them, they begin to understand some of the heart-breaking and challenging things the writer experienced. They try to track them down as they feel drawn towards them for some reason—you decide what. Where is the writer (character B) when character A finds them? How has their life developed since the journals ? How does character B react to them and the fact that they found the journals; why did the leave them behind? And what happens between these two characters unexpectedly love-wise when they get in contact? Heat and steam levels are up to you.

Story Outline:

22nd April

Situation: Character A is a well-known celebrity and in the public eye. They are famous for something you decide. One of their biggest critics is a well-known social media influencer and journalist; they constantly give the celebrity's work negative reviews. The celebrity is aware of their critique. Characters A and B come face to face when an interview is organised for the two of them, or at a public event to discuss character A's next masterpiece. What happens unexpectedly that leads to them becoming each other's love interest? This is an 'enemies to lovers' trope, heat and steam levels are up to you.

Story Outline:

23rd April

Situation: Let's write a fantasy romance featuring fairies. Fairy A has lost their way from their clan of fairies. What happens when she/he meets fairy B from a different breed, who is on the run for some reason, trying to escape their own fairy or mystical clan? The fairy B, who is on the run, has their elders looking for them, so they must move quickly. The lost fairy, A, has to make a decision on whether to go or not. If they do, what happens? Send them on a fairy-tale adventure in a mystical made up fantasy land! Turn them into lovers along the way with a beautiful HEA. Heat and steam levels are up to you.

Story Outline:

24th April

Situation: Let's write a Sci-Fi and futuristic love story. Choose your romance trope—enemies to lovers, second chance, forbidden love, friends to lovers etc, then create a story that's set one hundred years from now! Change the world as we know it. How does love and romance within your chosen trope look in the future? What are the challenges for your characters in this futuristic romance? Heat and steam levels are up to you.

Story Outline:

25th April

Person: Character A is a lonely soul, suffering from some kind of post-traumatic stress. One day while sitting on a bench at the park people watching and reflecting on their life, which feels empty, they start to contemplate suicide. A stranger (character B) takes a seat next to them and strikes up a conversation. This is what character A really needs right now, a friend, and they find it in this stranger's simple words and conversation. Character B can sense the tension with character A; what happens between these two? Create a romance that allows character A to come experience a U-turn on their suicidal thoughts, and character B to offer support and care. While all this is happening, cupid unexpectedly strikes from this random meeting that could be 'fated' and save one person's life. Heat and steam levels are up to you.

Story Outline:

26th April

Situation: Character A is a blogger who writes about their passions – you decide what they blog about. The blog has been running for maybe a year, but they feel they have no real response or engagement that has been consistent, so they're about to give up. When they don't blog for a while, someone (character B) starts to comment on all their posts and engage with them via their blog. They develop an unexpected fan via the Internet (character B), and engagement starts to pick up with new readers, current readers and character B, so they resume their blogging. Character B has been reading their blog all along and decided to engage when content was no longer shared. What happens between characters A and B? The blog is what connects them, what unexpected potential love develops? Who are these people in their daily lives? Heat and steam levels are up to you.

Story Outline:

27th April

Situation: Let's write a paranormal romance today. Character A crosses paths with a new love interest (character B) in an unexpected way. Character B is actually half human, half werewolf, fairy, witch or vampire etc. You decide, but character A doesn't know this. Character B is secretly living amongst humans in our realm. How do they meet? Where and why do they cross paths? What happens when character A finds out the truth in an unexpected way, and they're already emotionally invested? Heat and steam levels are up to you.

Story Outline

28th April

Situation: Character A, since childhood, has had 'visions' with a physic ability. As they matured into an adult this power dulled down, until they meet a love interest and become invested in them. Once they connect with character B, it's like the gateway to the other realm of powers they have is opened. They start to receive messages from the spirit realm and their psychic ability peaks. The visions are red flags of some sort or even positive messages you decide. This could be about character B and/or others. Why does character B naturally draw this ability out of character A? What happens? Character A is set on making this relationship work as it feels like a 'fated' love that came around unexpectedly when they weren't looking. Heat and steam levels are up to you.

Story Outline:

29th April

Situation: Let's write a romantic suspense today. Character A makes an instant connection with character B during a 'cute meet' you give them. Character B is hiding something as they were either a suspect or witness to a crime of your choice. Character B suddenly disappears. Character A feels ghosted but does some research and pieces together what Character B is hiding. They try to track them down, as they are in love. When they connect again what does character B do once character A confesses their love and devotion to them? How do these two characters deal with the situation that character A has been hiding all along? Create a twisty, page-turning suspenseful romance and bring these characters on a U-turn back in love. Heat and steam levels are up to you.

Story Outline:

30th April

Situations: What unexpected 'situation' have you had in love? Think back to an unexpected heart-break you've had. Today your challenge is to use that experience and turn it into a romance story with a HEA. Any genre, change names, heat and steam levels are up to you also.

Story Outline:

May

Historical, Regency and Multicultural

Welcome to May! This month let's try to create some beautiful, heartfelt, historical fiction stories. Here are some situations and people to guide you.

1st May

Situation: Character A is a war soldier (you decide which war, and what part of the world). They end up in hospital where his main carer (character B) is a nurse from a different background. What's her story, why is she in this part of the world? They fall for each other. How do they make this union work given their different backgrounds? Also with one of them responsible for the other's care, how does their romance play out? Heat and steam levels are up to you.

Story Outline:

2nd May

Situation: Character A is a southern man from the USA, and he has a change of heart over his actions as a slave master. He stops his involvement in the slave trade and instead he decides to help keep runaway slaves safe. Research and take a look at The Underground Railroad. He falls for one of the enslaved females he hides, but other slave masters find out. What happens in this forbidden love affair? Research well, and create a heart-felt story set in a very important historic period. Heat and steam levels are up to you.

Story Outline:

3rd May

Situation: Characters A and B are from different backgrounds, in an era when their relationship would have been frowned upon for whatever reason is relevant to them and the era. Maybe it's race, maybe it's status, maybe one is from a well-to-do family and the other is not. They had a short-lived secret romance, and character A leaves character B due to the stigma and fear of being found out. They regret it and try to come back to character B. However, their union is still frowned upon. Does character B have it in them to forgive, trust, and pick up where they left off? Can these two people in this 'forbidden love' stick together in the face of adversity? Allow them to find a way through it, bringing them on a U-turn and back in love, in the face of adversity against their union. Heat and steam levels are up to you and get creative!

Story Outline:

4th May

Situation: Set this story in the height of the witch hunt era, in any part of the world you wish, America or even Europe where it all took place. One of your characters has been accused of being a witch and practicing the craft. Her life is in danger—the local people of her town wish to kill her because they all believe she's a witch. One person who does not is the town's local outcast, recluse or strange person (character B). He offers to help her escape and they fall for each other during the preparations. On the run from their town to a new location where nobody knows them, how does their love develop? Do they both make it? And if they do, give them a HEA in a new location. For an extra twist, allow character A to actually be guilty of the crime: she is a witch a proud of it, but does she confess to character B? Research well; this could be a great love story in a very interesting historical period. Heat and steam levels are up to you.

Story Outline:

5th May

People: It's 'Cinco de Mayo,' a historical celebration held on this day to remember the successful battle the Mexican army had against the French. Today, craft a multicultural present date or historical romance story with a strong Mexican lead as a character. You can set the location of the story in Mexico or anywhere you wish, as long as one of your main characters is from this descent. Heat and steam levels are up to you.

Story Outline:

6th May

Situation: Character A is the daughter of a colonial governor of a Caribbean island who falls for a native on the island. How does this happen? How does the native react to her advances? What is their secret relationship like? Who discovers they have been getting close? Character A is put in a difficult position. She has tarnished the family name and maybe even is expecting a child if you decide this! Now she has to decide whether she'll give up her privilege and status for love with the island native. Heat and steam levels are up to you.

Story Outline:

7th May

Situation: Characters A and B are fighting for survival as a couple in an era of your choice. Character A immigrates to a country or an area of your choice. They set off to try to make a better life for them and their lover overseas or in a new location—you decide. Via letter exchanges, the couple remain in contact. Once your character arrives in their new destination they lose contact somehow with their lover, and letters stop after a while. Use letters to help tell the story. How does character B continue life and the struggle, what does character A do in their new location? Fifteen years (or however long you decide) later their paths cross. How and where do they meet again? And what happens when they meet? Heat and steam levels are up to you.

Story Outline:

8th May

Situation: Character A is a new maid or cook for a rich man with high status in society, or high-powered job in an era of your choice. The master of the house is pretty mean to all his servants, including the new maid. The maid does her job and stays out of his way, but one day he opens up to her about his grief. Why is he grieving ? What has made him so bitter since your maid has been employed? It could be a dark secret or something heart-felt. Link this grief in a very clever way to the maid's past somehow, and that draws them together. Or if you don't want this element of suspense, simply allow his opening up as a way to draw these two characters together. A secret affair starts, the other servants suspect something, and the word gets out. What happens in this love story? Heat and steam levels are up to you.

Story Outline:

9th May

People: Character A is a low paid secretary (or any profession you decide), and an African-American political activist in the 1960s-1970s. They cross paths with character B, who is white and in opposition against civil rights for African-Americans. Give them a 'cute meet' that's not so cute! They dislike each other, but soften towards each other. Character B is just following their family's traditional views. Somehow, they begin to want to prove each other wrong about the stereotypes they have of each other's race, they fall for each other. How does this happen? Create a story that shows lots of emotional push and pull from both sides, as well as a desire to get to know one another better as they break down stereotypes. Heat and steam levels are up to you.

Story Outline:

10th May

People: Character A is of Chinese descent, the time is between 1937 and 1945 during the Japanese occupation of China. Your character is a poor Chinese girl who loses touch with her family during this time as they flee for safety. Her parents, who are rebels against the Japanese, are captured then imprisoned. She is abandoned and on her own when a Japanese soldier (character B) hunting down Chinese rebels finds her and is struck by her beauty. Does he help her? How does their love develop during this politically charged time and their opposing backgrounds? Create a 'forbidden love' story during the Japanese occupation of China— research well this is very interesting history! Heat and steam levels are up to you.

Story Outline:

11th May

Situation: Character A is a total gossip and snob from a rich and wealthy background, in a historical period of your choice. They are a socialite and mix with the upper classes. They're popular but only because of the family they're from. Their parents are trying to find them a suitor. However, as they're such a free spirited and outspoken person rather than conservative, the upper-classed suitors are not that interested. They've had their eye on an eligible bachelor or bachelorette for some time, character B. Character B is being paired as suitor with their rival. In character A's diary they wrote brutally and honestly about their feelings about this—they hate *it* and their rival; they've even written lots of secret love letters that they haven't dared to mail to character B. The diary and letters are stolen, and the rival and character B find out about character A's feelings. What happens? Who stole the diary and letters? And why? Allow character A to find love somehow with character B, after a good dose of drama within the socialites and upper-classes! Heat and steam levels are up to you.

Story Outline:

12th May

Situation: Character A is a rich, upper-classed, character from whatever historical era you wish. Their family are encouraging them to marry, purely to maintain their good standing within their social circles and society. They don't want to marry, and are very happy to live the high life and gallivant. To keep their family quiet, they fake-propose to character B within their social circle, but have no real intentions of being a proper husband or wife. Character A lets character B know it's marriage for convenience, and even offers payment for the arrangement. Character B accepts it, they set the 'conditions of their marriage,' and character B allows character A to do as they please once they're married and live together. Character A falls for character B unexpectedly, even though they have an arrangement and character B has their own lover as part of the arrangement. Is it too late for character A to go back on their word? What happens in the marriage of convenience? Heat, steam and drama levels are up to you!

Story Outline:

13th May

Situation: An over-protective family from a wealthy, upper-class background and historical era of your choice, wants nothing but the best for their daughter—character A. They constantly introduce her to suitors but she is not interested. Character A's girlfriends bore her when they babble on about finding a wealthy man to settle down with in the social circles they move in. This changes when character A gets a glimpse of one of her father's associates—character B. What does character A do to get character B's attention? Character A confides in one of her girlfriends. Which one, and what happens? Character B is single and a wealthy man, but much older. Does character A's family approve of this union? Heat and steam levels are up to you.

Story Outline:

14th May

People: Character A is a soldier who has been called away to defend his country. character B is one of the many women from his home, or even a different country, who sends war soldiers letters in the mail to keep them company. They strike up an amazing connection. Who is she and what is her story? How does their love develop? And what is her life like while they are in contact? What happens when his service in the army is up? Give them a wonderful HEA that's heart-felt. Heat and steam levels are up to you.

Story Outline:

15th May

Situation: It's the end of the war in London, and character A's husband or wife died in a bomb strike. They're stuck down by grief and stress and they have three children to fend for. Character B also lost their family, who lives locally. Character A manages to connect with character B somehow. Both of them are suffering grief and PTSD but how they support each other through this, and the emotional push and pull leads to romance via their support system. Create lasting HEA for both of them. Heat and steam levels are up to you.

Story Outline

16th May

Situation: Set in a historical era of your choice, character A is a snobbish, very wealthy character in their mid-twenties. They are expected to marry a person of wealth, but they have turned their nose up at every suitor that has offered them marriage. Their parents have said 'this is the person.' This person– character B they have chosen is someone character A finds repulsive, as they are dominating, big-headed, arrogant and for themselves and their reputation. However, they are extremely highly regarded in society and is wealthy, and that's all that matters to character A and B's family. Their personalities clash as they are both alpha types. On the other hand, character B is sooooooo tasty and character A finds it hard to resist them. What happens as they are put together by their wealthy families? Heat and steam levels are up to you.

Story Outline:

17th May

People: Character A is an older, wealthy socialite and of status, in a historical era of your choice, and country of your choice. They are unmarried, without children, and believes it's too late for them to find a suitor at their age. They decide to travel and make the most of life, but they're deeply lonely. On their travels in this historical context, they find a stranger—character B. Character B offers character A much more than they bargained for. What happens in this love affair between a wealthy person of status in a historical setting and a foreigner (character B)? Heat and steam levels are up to you.

Story Outline:

18th May

People: In an historical era and location of your choice, character A is in deep mourning, as his wife passed away during labour or some tragic event of your choice, and so did the child. His business suffers, he isolates himself, fires all his staff and slowly goes on steady decline and turns to alcohol. His late wife's best friend gets in contact—character B. She literally barges into his life, as she heard the news about his business going under and his decline. Character B reminds character A of his late wife and it's so painful, he pushes her away and develops hate toward character B. Character B refuses to take no for an answer and tries get him back on his feet. Create a historical 'second chance love' story between these two, but allow conflicts for them too. Heat and steam levels are up to you.

Story Outline:

19th May

People: Set in a historical period of your choice, character A is broke as a joke. She's not from any kind of wealth and is a simple servant with nothing really fantastic about her, compared to the popular socialite women she works for. She's as 'common as muck' as us British would say. She decides to take her fate into her own hands; she wants and needs to change her lifestyle and status. She steals a dress from one of the wealthy ladies she tends to, convinced she'd never notice. Character A turns up to an event uninvited to secure herself a new future, and man. Who does she meet there? What happens, and does it go well? Does the wealthy lady notice her stolen dress? She crosses paths with character B, who of course is a man of wealth, what happens? Heat and steam levels are up to you.

Story Outline:

20th May

Situation: In a historical period of your choice, character A is the child of a highly respected family, and they are set to marry an equally wealthy and respected suitor that has been found. However, there's some kind of 'scandal' around the suitor's family, and character A's parents no longer sees them as fit to marry their child. A new person—character B, comes into the town or city for whatever reason you decide. Character A and character B start to court in private, and character A's parents agrees to the marriage finally. However, once married character A learns something about character B's past and where they have come from, the real reason they moved to the town or city think of something highly scandalous or even some kind of mystery. Character A's feelings about marriage start to change, they confide in their best friend who is a gossip among the socialites. What happens? Heat and steam levels are up to you.

Story Outline:

21st May

Situation: Character A is one of four children who are wealthy socialites, and highly respected. The person one of their siblings is interested—character B, has their eye on character A. Character A also has her eye on him, in secret. Who marries character B in the end? Heat, drama and steam levels are up to you.

Story Outline:

22nd May

People: Set in a historical era of your choice, character A is the wealthy, intelligent, handsome and sought-after son of a highly respected upper-classed family. Wealthy families have offered their daughter as a suitor left right and centre. None of the women really take his fancy, but he courts them casually anyway. He crosses paths with character B— an escort to upper-classed men, when he experiences her services. He falls for her and wishes to ask for her hand in marriage. How does he explain this to his wealthy family? How do they react to the news that he has been using escort services? What's their reaction to him wanting to marry a common escort? What does the escort—character B do? And how does this scandal vibrate through the upper classes and their tight, gossipy circles? Drama, heat and steam levels are up to you.

Story Outline:

23rd May

People: Today let's write an interracial romance! Set in any historical period you decide, your prompt is to create diversity in the historical romance genre. Use your imagination. Heat and steam levels are up to you.

Story Outline:

24th May

People: Today is World Schizophrenia Day. Your prompt is to simply create a romance story either historical, multicultural /interracial, or contemporary that features a main character who suffers from some form of mental ill-health. This does not have to be a deep and twisted character this is romance! Not a thriller. For character A, slight depression and PTSD impact on their day to day life. This leads them to spend time in a hospital for those who are experiencing mental ill-health. Here, character A finds romance and companionship with another patient, character B. Think of how mental ill-health may have been managed in the era you decide to set your story in and keep it relevant to that time. Get creative! Heat and steam levels are up to you.

Story Outline:

25th May

People: What is your own knowledge of myths and folklore in your own culture? If you have any idea, or are even slightly familiar, create a romantic historical story using folklore or myths from your own cultural background, or one you are drawn to. Heat and steam levels are up to you.

Story Outline:

26th May

Situation: Think of a historical event that you are really drawn to, familiar with, or would like to know more about. Research it, gather the facts, then create two characters that meet during this event. What happens? Do they have a HEA or HFN? Heat and steam levels are up to you.

Story Outline:

27th May

People: Create two characters who become romantically connected in the 1950s. Who are they? How did they meet? What is their background, and what conflicts do they experience as individual people? How do their paths cross? What adventures do they have relevant to this era? Do they have a HEA or HFN? Heat and steam levels are up to you.

Story Outline:

28th May

People: Create two characters who become romantically connected in the 1920s. Who are they? How did they meet? What is their background, and what conflicts do they have as individual people? How do their paths cross? What adventures do they have relevant to this era? Do they have a HEA or HFN? Heat and steam levels are up to you.

Story Outline:

29th May

People: Create two characters who become romantically connected from the 1970s. Who are they? How did they meet? What is their background, and what conflicts do they have as individual people? How do their paths cross? What adventures do they have relevant to this era? Do they have a HEA or HFN? Heat and steam levels are up to you.

Story Outline:

30th May

Situation: In an era of your choice, character A is promised to someone else as a marriage partner. For character A, a person they would love court and get to know—character B, suddenly becomes single (for whatever reason you give them). What's character A's next move, do they try to get themselves out of the current arrangement and promise for marriage, now that character B is single? Or is there some kind of love triangle? Heat and steam levels are up to you.

Story Outline:

31st May

Situation: Today is all about *your history*. Think back to how your romantic life has been, the good, the bad and the ugly. Pick a situation you have experienced then place this into an actual plot. You can use all or some of your situational experience, and of course change the *era,* culture, and names of people. The point is to draw upon your own historical experiences and create a fresh new plot that's historical romance. Heat and steam levels are up to you.

Story Outline:

June

Contemporary Romance

Welcome to June. This month let's create some fresh, engaging and realistic contemporary romance stories. Contemporary romance tends to haves strong characters that are very well developed, so good they jump out of the pages, and set in the modern day. I'd encourage you to set your stories in interesting places and include as many 'real life' events and as much realism as you can.

1st June

People: At the start of the academic year in September character A, a high school teacher, has a new student. They are withdrawn, slightly behind in their abilities, and show signs of being a child who needs some professional help. You decide the trauma for this student and how deep it is, and what happened in their most recent past. Character A contacts their parent, who is a single parent—either a mother or father—that's new to the city or town. There is an attraction between the two, but it's a line they don't know whether to cross. The child's well-being brings the two together, as the child has a hard time adjusting and overcoming whatever past trauma you give them. Character A gives additional learning support and emotional support to the child and parent. What happens with these two? Heat and steam levels are up to you.

Story Outline:

2nd June

Situation: Character A works in a professional corporate environment that is competitive and cut-throat. They are single and really focused on their career and moving up. They meet their CEO's son (or daughter) at an event, and start ranting about how they work their ass off and don't get the recognition they feel they deserve, and they bad-mouth the company. The two are attracted to each other regardless. Character A doesn't know that character B is related to the big boss but, they find out when they have their first date. What happens between these two characters? Heat and steam levels are up to you.

Story Outline:

3rd June

Situation: It's World Bicycle Day today in many parts of the world. Character A is a bicycle lover and regularly goes riding. They've recently moved to a new city, as they broke up with their ex and sold the property they had together. They look online for activities to do with biking and go on a meet-up for a local bike ride. Here they cross paths with character B. Character B has a nasty accident on their bike at the first event they attend, and character A comes to their assistance. Character B has trust issues since their last break up. How do these two develop a romance that's 'second chance,'? keep in mind they both have baggage from past relationships. Heat and steam levels are up to you.

Story Outline:

4th June

Situation: Character A has a love-hate relationship with one of their co-workers— character B. They work in the same building or department. For some reason they just rub each other the wrong way as people. What happened between them? You decide. One day, character A enters the lift on the way up to the floor they work on, it's just character A and B in the lift when there's a power cut in the building and the lift gets stuck for a while. What happens when they are stuck in each other's space for a couple of hours? Once they are rescued from the lift and the power comes back on, continue the cat and mouse story between them, and bring them together. Heat and steam levels are up to you.

Story Outline:

5th June

Situation: Characters A and B met online and are trying to have a long-distance relationship. They can be in different countries, states, towns, etc. They fall in love even though they have never met. However, they have some struggles when it comes to meeting in person for the first time—something 'major' happens to stop this meet up. They try to continue their relationship, but character A gets bored. They feel character B is complacent and not really trying, so they start to move on. They still have not meet in person due whatever is standing in their way. Can character B convince character A, who seems to be moving on, that their love is worth the fight even though they have not met yet? What happens with this situation? Is there a HEA or does one of them move on and the other lives in regret? Do they ever finally meet? When and how? Heat and steam levels are up to you.

Story Outline:

6th June

People: Characters A and B are in a failing marriage. They married each other quickly maybe, without really knowing each other that well. She married him for his 'potential' as a husband, and he married her as she felt like his 'security.' How do they bring their marriage back on track? Do they stray from their marriage? Who is fighting the hardest and how does the other react? Heat and steam levels are up to you.

Story Outline:

7th June

Situation: "If I could meet him/her again, I'd tell them that…"
Character A has something to say to character B. If they could turn
back time what would they say, or have done, differently? Heat and
stem levels are up to you.

Story outline:

8th June

People: It's World Ocean Day around the world. Characters A and B meet by the ocean, river, pond, a marine life centre or some location that is surrounded by water. The location is anywhere in the world you wish—local, for away, exotic, etc. Each day around the same time character A appears here and character B notices them. What is it about this location that is so meaningful to character A, why do they go there often? What is character B doing there also? For whatever reason you give them, allow character A to black out on one of their visits and character B comes to their rescue. If character B were not there this person would have surely died! Once rescued, allow these characters to get to know each other's back story and develop a lasting love with some push and pull, conflict or even suspense along the way. The water or location is central and important to them both. Heat and steam levels are up to you.

Story Outline:

9th June

Situation: Today let's write a billionaire romance. Character A is a rich, wealthy billionaire of the modern world. They could be a businessman/woman or makes their money legitimately and legally in some other way, which has landed him/her in a very financially secure position. When a change in the economic environment puts their business at risk, their business starts to suffer, and they call in a financial consultant or manager to help liquidate some of their assets to generate cash. This consultant—character B—is a surprise to them. Not only are they stunning, very confident and witty, they're one of character A's previous partners whom they broke off an engagement with five years ago in order to focus on building their business. What happens when their paths cross and character B now realises character A's business is suffering, after they left to make a fortune? Can character B forgive character A and help them, or does character B pass the case to a co-worker to deal with? How do they handle their first face to face meeting? Heat and steam levels are up to you.

Story Outline:

10th June

People: Character A is a businesswoman/man who has very little time for themself. They consult a match-making agency in hopes of finding love with a man/woman equality as financially stable, intelligent and caring as they are. What happens when the matchmaker— character B, takes an interest in character A's application and profile for match-making services? Does character B set character A up with men/women who they think will stand a low chance with character A, so character B can have character A as a love interest? Does character B cross the line and make their interest in character A known? Heat and steam levels are up to you.

Story Outline:

11th June

Situation: Summer love! It's almost mid-June and summer is in full swing in many parts of the world. Characters A and B are moving forward in life, from something or someone they wish to cut ties with. Separately, they take summer holidays to the same beautiful destination in the world. Do your research and send them on a summer love affair somewhere hot, exotic and beautiful. Where, how, and when do they meet during their vacation? How do they pass the time together? And does it last just the duration of the holiday, or do they end up together for the longer term after some doubts over whether it can really work as it's a holiday romance? Heat and steam levels are up to you.

Story Outline:

12th June

Situation: Summer love, part two, following yesterday's prompt. Character A is an air hostess/host. On one of their flights they randomly bump into one of their old flames. Both of them have changed since they first their first relationship together. You decide why and how they have changed, along with why they originally broke up. Neither of them got married following the break-up. One of them slips the other their contact details as the flight lands. What happens next when they land in their destination? Rekindle their romance, allow them to catch up on lost time and possibly try again. Give them challenges, push and pull, lots of emotions and a lovely ending. Heat and steam levels are up to you.

Story Outline:

13th June

Situation: Character A's friend sets them up on a blind date, after they have been looking for love for a while and single for a year. You decide how their friend encourages them to go. On the date character A is not really that keen on the person; there's a personality clash or just no real chemistry. However, while character A and their date are at the bar, the bartender takes a fancy to character A and overhears the conversation. It's clear it's a blind date that's not going well. The bartender – character B slips— character A a note when their date goes to the bathroom. How does this potential love triangle go? Character A debates whether to make contact. When they do, what happens? Heat and steam levels are up to you.

Story Outline:

14th June

Situation: Character A feels that they are totally unworthy of love. This is due to something they did in the past, or that happened to them. It could be a crime, a lie, cheating, etc and it resulted in the loss of their former life as they knew it; their world crashed down. Character A is not in a good head space overall, and they are plodding through life with no real aim or passion. Someone from their past (character B), whom they had to abandon, returns. Character B finds character A in a low place. Is their return welcomed by character A? How do their worlds collide again this time around? Keep it as suspenseful as you like! Heat and steam levels are up to you.

Story Outline:

15th June

Situation: Character A's mother and only living parent is on her death bed and will pass away soon, for whatever reason you decide. Character A's mother hands her a letter and confesses that character A's father was not her first true love; there was another man. Once she passes away peacefully, character A opens the letter – what does it say? What did her mother want her first love and character A to know before she died? Character A tracks down the man. He is suffering with serious dementia and therefore recalls very little, but character A gets to know his child—character B and love develops, how? And where does it lead given that Character A's and B's parents were once in love, and Character A's mother has passed and it's only a matter of time before Character B's father passes also. Heat and steam levels are up to you.

Story Outline:

16th June

Situation: At the coffee shop one morning, character A stumbled and spilt coffee over character B. It's the start of a new romance! Who is character B? What is their reaction and how does this lead to romance? Heat, steam or even comedy levels are up to you!

Story Outline:

17th June

People: Character A is a confident, and maybe even snobbish character who starts a new job, then takes part in a team building week away in a location of your choice. They are paired with the IT geek (character B). Do opposites really attract? If they do in your world, show the character development as character A goes from 'no thanks' to 'yes please!' Heat and steam levels are up to you.

Story Outline:

18th June

Situation: Romantic comedy day! 'The accidental boyfriend/girlfriend,' character A, takes a trip to Paris for whatever reason you give them. They need to spend extended time there. They meet Character B, get to know them and start dating or have a date. Character A shares a kiss with character B, not realising that in French culture such things are only for when two people wish to go 'steady.' Character A has misunderstood the difference in dating culture, and now is in a 'relationship' but doesn't realise it. What happens between these two people given their different dating styles, cultures and assumptions made about their relationship status? Heat, steam and comedy levels are up to you.

Story Outline:

19th June

Situation: Character A is a female who is always running late for her appointments for whatever reason you decide. She's caught speeding by the same traffic cop more than once, there's attraction. What happens between these two? Heat and steam levels are up to you.

Story Outline:

20th June

People: It's World Refugee Day. Character A is a refugee to a new country. You decide where they are coming from, where they have arrived, and why. As part of their settling-in program they have a social worker to assist them. They are suffering with settling, past trauma and maybe even finding it hard to see light at the end of the tunnel. Their social worker becomes overwhelmed with their caseload and refers them to a special weekly group to help settle in and meet a support network. Who does your refugee meet there who helps them to settle in, and also falls for them and their vulnerability? (This is character B). Whoever they meet, character B does not have an easy time because character A is not that trusting. How does character B break down character A's barriers from this weekly contact at the support group, to allow love to blossom and a new life to start for character A? Make this a heart-felt romance with all the 'feels' of emotion and character development. Heat, steam and suspense are up to you!

Story Outline:

21st June

People: It's International Yoga Day. Character A gave up her well-paying job against the advice of friends and family and her ex-partner who didn't support her desire to do what makes her happy. She quit her nine-to-five and opened a yoga studio. The studio is struggling to gain new members to her class, but she is determined to prove her critics wrong and make it work. She does a marketing campaign to get people through the door. They start to flood in, and in walks her first male participant—character B. He takes up yoga to help with recovery from an old injury to his back, or maybe to regain balance in his own life – you decide. He requests one-to-one lessons. Attraction sparks. What happens between them? What are their past conflicts they are trying to overcome as people? And how does their enjoyment of yoga connect them? Heat and steam levels are up to you.

Story Outline:

22nd June

People: Often romance is focused on the younger market. Create characters in their more senior years placed in a modern-day setting looking for love, or who unexpectedly find love. For example, the Internet connects in seconds people who are on the other side of the world. For someone aged over sixty, how might they find the experience of online dating in their more senior years? Or how about if they were to keep it old school and answered an advert in the paper for a 'companion', or even a pen pal... heat and steam levels are up to you.

Story Outline:

23rd June

Situation: Character A is a police officer responsible for a female, currently in police protection. He goes over and above his job to protect her, and he develops an infatuation and desire for her. Why is she—character B, in police protection? How and why is this police offer drawn to her? What happens when his feelings take over and he is pushed to overstep the line of duty and show her how he really feels? How does she react? Heat, steam and even suspense levels are up to you.

Story Outline:

24th June

Situation: Character A is an aspiring writer and has a day job. They decide to take a creative writing course part time to help improve their craft during the evenings after work. The teacher— character B, is appealing. Character A starts to write little 'love notes' and poems to the teacher, and the teacher finds them when character A hands them in accidently with an assignment...what happens next? Heat, steam and comedy levels are up to you.

Story Outline

25th June

Situation: It's romantic suspense day! Characters A and B get to know each other and quickly decide they want to make it official. A few days after they decide to make it 'official,' character A's phone is non-responsive, character B can't get hold of them and they lose contact as character A just disappears. Character B tries desperately to track them down. Unsuccessful, they try to move on with life. A few months later character B receives a message from character A on social media, telling them they do love them, they mean it, but 'something came up.' What happened to character A? Where are they now? Contact reduces again, and a few months later character A reappears in character B's life somehow, but is it too late? Character B is unsure if they meant it when character A said they love them. What's the deal with the disappearing act? How does character A convince character B they do love them, it was always them they wanted but something 'came up.' Heat, steam and suspense levels are up to you.

Story Outline:

26th June

Situation: Romantic crime thriller day! Character A is a happy-go-lucky person, enjoys life and is generally doing well. They are from a small town and yearn for some excitement in life. You create where they are at in life now, job, friends etc. They meet character B at the scene of a crime. What was the crime? Why are they both in this location? This crime connects them and starts a crazy love affair. Heat and steam levels are up to you.

Story Outline:

27th June

Situation: Character A is either on holiday, a short trip, or back-packing around the world. You decide. Give them a reason to be in this new location. Make the location somewhere interesting, with a lot of attractions—either a city or town, wherever you wish. Love blooms when they head into a tourist shop to buy a map, then lock eyes with the person who serves them at the counter. How do they spark off a conversation, how do they meet again? Give them lovely, fun, romantic story in this great location.

Story Outline:

28th June

People: Romantic comedy day! Both your characters are coffee addicts. When there is a major sale such as Black Friday at the local stores, both of your characters have in mind that they want a new coffee machine. While shopping they both grab the last box on the shelf. Annoyed, they both turn to each other. What do they say? Who claims it? And how does this encounter turn into a first date just from their love of coffee? Heat, steam and comedy levels are up to you.

Story Outline:

29th June

Situation: It all started with an accidental text: character A sent a text message to character B's phone. One digit was wrong and it was meant for someone else. What was the message? What made character B want to respond? How does the text marathon between these two spark a first date and love affair? Who are these people in their current lives and what conflicts are they dealing with romantically? What are their goals? Are their goals in sync or opposing? Heat and steam levels are up to you.

Story Outline:

30th June

People: Character A is so serious about finding love and marriage, they consider a mail order bride. How do they land themselves in this position? What has happened to make them consider this route to find a marriage partner? Who do they find? What country are they from? What about the bride—character B? What made her decide to become a bride? Did she ever think she'd be selected? Give them some adventures! Heat, steam and comedy levels are up to you.

Story Outline:

July

Paranormal, Horror and Dark Romance

Welcome to July! Things get a little dark and supernatural this month! I've never really been naturally drawn to this genre as a writer, until I co-authored a book and found it incredibly hard! But enjoyable. But as a reader, I lap up paranormal romance and really enjoy some of it. Here's some story ideas to get the juices flowing. Remember heat and steam levels are up to you, and you can also use these prompts for other genres, just remove the paranormal aspects.

1st July

Situation: Character A stumbles across a 'book of spells' hidden in their late mother's attic, as they clear the house to prepare it for sale. Along with the book of spells are a large box with all kinds of witchy things, and an Ouija board. Your character is shocked as they never would have thought her mother would be interested in esoteric things. Character A doesn't say anything to their siblings, but they take the box, book and board home. They're intrigued and have been single for a while, so they carry out a love ritual as per the book (research this if need be), and their ex-shows up! What happens? Did the spell go wrong or right? How does your character react, and what does their ex want? Heat and steam levels are up to you.

Story Outline:

2nd July

People: Character A has a fascination with 'the other side' and death, but not to the point that they're morbid. They've just never really feared death, or the dead. Maybe they are a funeral director or some kind of grief councillor—you decide their job. To the outside person, they look pretty 'average' and no one would guess that they'd love to explore what it would be like to become immortal—to die, but still be alive. Character B is a vampire who crosses paths with your human character A somehow. This meeting happens at the dead of night. Where are they? Does character A realise who and what they have stumbled on? What happens between them romantically? Character A has a fascination with all that character B is—dead...but also alive! Heat and steam levels are up to you.

Story Outline:

3rd July

People Characters A and B are average, everyday people but have a fascination with ghosts. They meet while on a ghost hunting session, either in a house that is claimed to be haunted, or the cemetery. It's an 'insta connection' feeling. The moment they spoke they were intrigued by each other. Together they enjoy the ghost hunting session and meet again on the next one. How does this spooky love affair develop? What does their date night look like? Give them regular jobs if you want and a 'normal set up' in their life, but how did the fascination with the spirit world start? They both have a backstory on this. Heat and steam levels are up to you.

Story Outline

4th July

Situation: Character A is suffering from some kind of grief or trauma. They lost a love one in a terrible, tragic, almost-freak accident. In spirit their loved one watches over them and sees that they really are not moving on in life. Character A has joined a grief management group. Here they meet another grieving soul—character B. Together, they work through it and find love with each other with the help of character A's loved one as their spirit guide. Heat and steam levels are up to you, but make this a very uplifting, heart-felt and even spooky at times story with loads of wonderful paranormal activity, to guide these two souls to happiness.

Story Outline:

5th July

Situation: Create a world where there are different species of beings: witches, fairies or anything you feel drawn too. There are some that are good, bad, evil and everything in between. Character A hunts down vampires, as they hate them and need to get rid of as many of them in order for their people or species to survive. They are simply prey for vampires. Character A, the ring-leader of their people, is put in a very difficult position when they come across a vampire that they are attracted to for some strange reason—you decide the reason. What happens? And how does this world change, when the ruler over the vampire slayer species (character A) falls for their prey , that they are normally against sharing any form of space or land with. Allow character A to learn the ins and outs of how the vampire species really operates and allow them to realise that they had them all wrong, discriminating against them all these hundreds or even thousands of years. Heat and steam levels are up to you.

Story Outline:

6th July

People: Hunting for witches can be dangerous. Character A is human. They decide to go snooping in the woods one night, convinced that there's a group of witches and wizards that gather in the woods each full moon. What happens when character A is on the hunt for the witches and wizards, but is captured by a witch or wizard, then whisked off to another land? They wake up in their own bed in a cold sweat. Was the experience real or just a dream? They cross paths with the same witch or wizard that captured them in this realm—character B. It could be via work, a dating site, or any location or situation you decide. When they meet, how does an unexpected and unusual romance between them start? And again, was it all dream? How do they recognise the person that captured them? Heat and steam levels are up to you.

Story Outline:

7th July

People: Every full moon something strange happens in character A's town, or location you create. Character A takes it upon themselves to check it out, but never finds much even though they hear the howls, screams and strange things going on from their window. One full moon they head deeper into the woods and a wolf appears, then changes into their human form. Character A can't be sure, but they could have sworn it was someone they know—character B. Who was it? Character A becomes obsessed with character B as they know them, and wish to get to the bottom of what they saw. When they do, they realise that character B has some kind of 'super ability,' and they experience it with them, maybe even in another realm. Bring these two together in a twisty love story between a human and a hybrid wolf and human who has something to hide. Heat and steam levels are up to you.

Story Outline:

8th July

Situation: In 19th century England, character A takes a job working as a live-in maid. The owner of the house is rather strange. He mostly keeps to himself and is the owner of a pub. The gossip from the other housekeepers is that many people have been reluctant to work for him, as the house is haunted. Character A is desperate for a job, and not from a wealthy background so she took the job. Part of the house is never to be entered, according the housekeepers. One day she hears strange noises from that wing of the house. She also notices strange women coming and going at night, and the same noises of pain and pleasure coming from that wing of the house. Character B— the landlord has a kinky, sexual, fetish that character A has never experienced. He is also a vampire or some kind of creature of the night— whatever you wish to make him. Character A's innocence and curiosity intrigue character B. Character A is intrigued by the noises she hears and her boss. Bring them together in a spooky, erotic, kinky, love story. Heat and steam levels are up to you but this could make a wonderful steamy paranormal story.

Story Outline:

9th July

People: Character A is moving away to a new location and has purchased a house. They could have decided to move away due to trauma, a break-up or received an inheritance of money— whatever reason you decide. The house is very old, set back on a hill, with some land attached to it. Even though it's old, this is what attracts character A to it, as they wish to spend time revamping the house. Create their new life in this new location— friends, trying to date and finding love, etc. Character A hires a decorator—character B, to help with the redecorations. When they strip the wallpaper they notice messages that have been written. Both characters are intrigued and start to investigate who left them. But the more they dig, it's almost like they are receiving 'warnings' to stay away and not dig up the past, as strange things happen in the house and to both of them. It does not stop them; this new project brings the two characters together, along with all the paranormal activity. Character A feels unsafe and character B wants to protect them. Create a horror or paranormal love story where this strange house, messages on the wall, and activity in the house and on the land becomes very serious and life threatening. This draws characters A and B together, as they want to get to the bottom of it all and understand the messages on the walls. Heat and steam levels are up to you.

Story Outline:

10th July

Situation: Character A is a news reporter, journalist, a true crime writer, or maybe even just an investigator of crimes as they have an interest. There's been a gruesome murder at a house that, as far as everyone in the town is aware, is normally abandoned. There's rumours that it's haunted, too. Character B—the detective assigned to the case, is pretty hot, but character A does not really get along with them. They always have a harsh way with the media and crime investigators. Every time character B crosses paths with character A, when they are trying to get some information for writing about crimes that happen in the city, character B is abrupt. Character A is at the house when everyone is gone. Out of interest, character B also goes back to check out the scene. As character B drives by, they hear character A's screams echo around the area. Character B has to save Character A, what happens when Character B enters the house? Create a horror or paranormal story with a touch of romance, give these two opposing characters a whirlwind romance with push and pull when character B saves character A. Character A's grateful character B shows up but in character A's eyes character B's still an ass…Character B now sees character A differently once they save them.

Story Outline:

11th July

People: Characters A and B have a 'cute meet.' Show their relationship developing and give them any conflicts you choose. Character A has trust issues, Character B is trying hard to gain their trust, so that character A will fully invest in the relationship. Maybe character B wants marriage or to move forward to the next level. Just when things seem to be on track, the spirit of character B's dead ex starts making themselves known. Character A finds out a nasty secret about how character B's ex died, and Character B was involved. It was a Ouija board session that went wrong, or even some form of dark sex game or BDSM that went wrong. How does this new paranormal activity that's disrupting both of their lives pan out for them? Allow them to experience a U-turn, and end up with a HEA. Send the spirit towards the 'light' so it stops bothering them. Heat, steam and suspense levels are up to you.

Story Outline:

12th July

People: It's Friday the 13th when characters A and B meet. where and how do they collide? Why are they both in this place at the same time? Give them a feeling of 'insta connection' in an unusual setting as they are both very unusual characters—into things witchy, esoteric, mysterious and even downright dangerous! Or if you're stuck, allow them to meet at a creepy themed masquerade ball. Character A is suffering from a broken heart and finding their way back into the world and gaining confidence. You decide what happened to them in the past. When they meet on Friday the 13th, they connect over this common ground they have, with a love of the strange and unusual. Character B asks character A out for a drink, they accept and they meet up. From here, character B is more into 'unusual fetishes' than character A is, and slowly character B introduces them to some new things in and out of the bedroom. Something goes wrong as they carry out character B's fetishes. Character A loses their confidence and trust in character B, they literally try to cut them off and become scared. Allow character B to work at gaining their trust, bring them back to a happy safe place where they can carry out their fetishes. Heat and steam levels are up to you.

Story Outline:

13th July

Situation: For characters A and B, it's character B's birthday or they have achieved some kind of milestone set. Character A buys character B a wonderful watch or item of jewellery, that they found at a second-hand shop to celebrate. As soon as the watch or jewellery arrives in their house their relationship takes a turn for the worse. What happens? As character B wears the item, they have a near death experience and recalls the original owner's fate and death. How did they die? What happens next when their lives are turned upside down by this item, and it causes them to split up? Once character B realises the item's negative energy, how do they try to convince character A to come back? It was not character B acting 'strange' it was caused by the item's negative vibrations. Together, character A and B piece together what they know about the original owner of the watch, jewellery or item, close the mystery and 'curse,' then put it behind them. They become a stronger couple with a HEA. Heat and steam levels are up to you.

Story Outline:

14th July

Situation: Write a story about a couple who meet in an online forum created specially to find partners, to practice BDSM or a sub-dom relationship. They have everyday lives and you can create an environment and set up for them that you are drawn to. Also, give them some past conflicts or areas of their character to develop as people. They get to know each other casually and attraction is there. Build the heat, but together they agree to keep this as strictly business to explore their desires that led them to the forum in the first place. This 'practice' or agreement turns into a romantic affair, when character A wants more. What does character B do? How do they break their 'agreement' to start a romance that is based on love as well, and learn to have relationships that are based on love and not just control and submission? This is the obstacle they must overcome: how to 'love' and be 'loved' outside of their dark sexual desires or need for a sub-dom relationship. Heat and steam levels are up to you.

Story Outline:

15th July

People: In Victorian London, a man learns that his new wife has been holding back a secret. She said she had 'no living family.' He never realised exactly what she meant by this. Her family are vampires or some creature of the night that are immortal— dead, but alive. How does this love affair continue? How and why did they even get married? Why is she not a creature of the night too, or is she? You decide. What happens now the secret is out? Give them some challenges and strains to test their marriage and love, but bring them to a HEA or HFN. Heat, steam and suspense levels are up to you.

Story Outline:

16th July

People: Simple task today: create a romantic story with heat/suspense levels of your choice between a human and a shifter. Allow them to meet in this realm. Character A actually sees character B shift into something, let's say an object of some kind. Character A decides to take that object home with them! What happens next? Heat and steam levels are up to you.

Story Outline:

17th July

Situation: Let's write a romance story with a touch of horror. Character A is having very vivid dreams about the gruesome death of their ex-partner, or an old friend. They are currently in a new relationship, but they decide to see if they can track down their ex or old friend, only to find that they really have died. How does this put a strain on their current relationship? Why did they decide to track them down? What do they find out about their death? Is it linked to them or to something they promised them before they broke up? Heat, steam and suspense levels are up to you.

Story Outline:

18th July

People: Character A is a psychic, and also reads tarot and oracle cards. They are a very eccentric character and deeply into magical arts and all things esoteric. They don't really like dating that much, as they can foresee what may happen with the romantic interests they meet. A client (character B) comes to them for a psychic reading, and character A suddenly realises that they have a connection to them, and the same tarot card that they keep on drawing out when they do their own readings appears in the reading for the client—character B. What happens, where does this situation lead to? Bring these two people together in a twisty, strange and even shocking story that leads possibly to closure, or a HEA that character A deserves. Put character A out of their misery over why they won't date, their past or something they are holding on to in life somehow. Allow character B to be central to this. Heat and steam levels are up to you.

Story Outline:

19th July

Situation: Think of the most creepy and scary location you can imagine. Now, put character A there. What are they doing there? Whatever they are doing, they cross paths with character B. What are they doing there? Make this a creepy 'love at first sight' or 'insta connection' story based on the reason these two people are at this location. Why can't they now leave each other alone? Lastly, give them some kind of obstacle or conflict over why they should not really be together, but by the end of the story they are together. Heat, steam, suspense or creepiness are all up to you.

Story Outline:

20th July

Situation: Today, it all starts with a phone call. This can be paranormal, horror, urban fantasy, whatever you wish the genre to be. 'It all started with a phone call.' Character A receives a phone call in the dead of the night, maybe it woke them up, maybe they were waiting for it—you decide. What's so deadly about this contact made with them, via phone? How does this play a role in what happens next, or who they meet which leads to romance? The trope can be 'fated' 'enemies to lovers' 'second chance' etc. Whatever you want, just make it happen with a phone call. Heat, steam and suspense levels are up to you.

Story Outline:

21st July

People: Character A has been stuck in a haunted castle, or house for many years. Why have they been held there? And by whom? What happened? This is character A. Character B is their long-lost love, who they left when they were confined to the castle. Character B now has new information about their whereabouts, and they are on the hunt for them. What happens? This can be any genre you wish, paranormal, horror, fantasy, etc. Heat and steam levels are up to you.

Story Outline:

22nd July

People: In a fantasy setting, character A is a 'gentle giant' of some sort who is often feared. They are lonely as there are not many of their kind, but they are looking for companionship. They make friends with a fairy or some creature that's much more delicate, and normally would be very scared of him. How does their friendship start? What are your characters bonding over given that they are opposites? Create an 'opposites attract' love story with two very contrasting characters and show how they overcome their prejudgement of each other, to find companionship that's lasting. Heat and steam levels are up to you.

Story Outline:

23rd July

Situation: Write a story about the 'end of time' coming. There is about to be a change in the fantasy or paranormal world that you have created. Character A is in distress. What happened ? Why are they worried about the 'end of time' coming, what are their motives, and what must they do? Character B is character A's saviour, though character A does not know it. Character B comes to their rescue during all the chaotic events that are happening, or about to happen as the 'end of time' draws near. How does character A react, do they push character B away, not believe them, or embrace them? Heat and steam levels are up to you.

Story Outline:

24th July

People: Write a story about a child who has not crossed over to the other side; they are roaming this realm in spirit form. Why are they still here? How did they die? They start to follow a human—character A who longs for children. What does this spirit child do to make their presence known in this human's life? They connect their human—character A with character B, who is a struggling single parent. Make this a story of 'fated meetings' using this ghost child as the force that brings them together somehow. Heart-felt paranormal romance! Heat and steam levels are up to you.

Story Outline:

25th July

Situation: Character A is in some form of danger due to their blood line. They possess something 'magical' that others want. Character A has managed to avoid capture for a long time, as they have been on the run. What happens when they land themselves in a new location and cross paths with a love interest—character B. However, this love interest is on a secret mission to capture character A for the 'magical' blood line they possess. Character B is in a situation of conflict between their head (the mission they are on) and heart (the feelings that they are developing), when they realise character A appeals to them. Character A is not aware that character B is on a secret mission. What happens between these two? Heat and steam levels are up to you.

Story Outline:

26th July

People: Character A discovers they have a 'superpower' of some sort, that's been unleashed within them. They want to use it to find a companion and change their life. What are their motives now they have this power? What have they been struggling with that is now possible? This character can be a human who now realises they are 'superhuman.' They have their eye on someone forbidden—their boss, a friend etc. What do they do to get what they want when it comes to love and life, and what happens? Heat and steam levels are up to you.

Story Outline:

27th July

Situation: Character A is a police officer or some kind of law enforcement. They have character B as a suspect for something— you decide what, and have detained them. Character B is a shifter and escapes the law. What they don't know is that character A, the law enforcement character, is also a shifter they use their abilities and mange to catch up with character A. How does character A go about managing their duty as a law enforcement officer, and their own secret vs their heart, when they realise that their 'own kind' are still very much alive? Character B catches feelings for character A, who is also a wanted suspect for something. What happens? Heat, steam and suspense levels are up to you.

Story Outline:

28th July

People: Write a story featuring the sea underworld. Character A is actually partly mermaid. She often comes into the human world with her human legs (think of the movie Splash if you have seen it). This could be because she is not really accepted fully in the sea world, as she is part human. Create her experiences in both worlds. A lonely fisherman—character B notices her one day as she comes up from the sea, but she does not notice him watching. He thinks he imagined her and dismisses it until he meets her again when he has a nasty accident while fishing, character A is near and helps him. What happens between these two? Give this mermaid a love interest she deserves, due to her difficulty in her natural sea world, and fascination with the human world. Heat and steam levels are up to you.

Story Outline:

29th July

Situation: Character A is a female warrior in a world that you create. She is one of many who are fighting against the takeover of their land, and resources. She comes face to face with the ring leader of the opposition—character B, a horrible person. She has the chance to kill him, he begs her not to as for him it's 'love at first sight.' How does this happen? Does she use her sword to finish him or does she let him go, and regrets it due to her loyalty to her people? Does she fall for him? Her distrust of him and his motives is high, as he is the ring leader of the opposition. Create a love story with plenty of feelings, emotion and even growth as the two characters fight to get what they want, when their goals are originally very different and focused on the interest of their own people. Heat and steam levels are up to you.

Story Outline:

30th July

Situation: It's International Friendship Day today. Create a story where this is the main element. A 'friends to lovers' story or a story where friendship is found for two very lonely people. You decide the genre—paranormal, horror, fantasy etc—but friendship must be the main plot driver. How do your characters become friends? Why have they crossed paths? And how does this lead to a soul mate connection for them. Or they are already friends, and this moves in a new direction? Heat and steam levels are up to you.

Story outline:

31st July

Situation: Using a romantic experience you've had before in your life, place this in a supernatural, paranormal or horror context! Heat and steam levels are up to you.

Story Outline:

August

Christmas and Holiday Love!

Welcome to August, writer, and I know what you're probably thinking Christmas and holiday stories in August? Yep, that's right. If you focus on them early, you stand a good chance of releasing a story or two to the world this coming Christmas and holiday season. I actually wrote my first ever Christmas story in August, so let's get started.

1st August

Situation: Characters A and character B are co-workers, but they don't have a great dynamic between them— you decide why that is. What happens when they draw each other's name out of the Secret Santa hat at a team-building event? How does this love-hate working relationship develop into something meaningful over Christmas, and Secret Santa? Heat and steam levels are up to you.

Story Outline:

2nd August

Situation: Another spin on 'Secret Santa' gifting often done within many workplaces. Characters A and B have their own individual wants, needs, goals, past hurts, etc. Give them both something they need to work on as people. What happens when they randomly pull each other's name out of the hat as a Secret Santa? Create your own happy ever after, steamy, or contemporary romance where the 'luck' of them meeting, is purely down to Secret Santa gifting. These two characters provide each other with what they need, to deal with their individual wants, needs, goals, past hurts etc. Heat and steam levels are up to you.

Story Outline:

3rd August

People: Character A has been receiving little love notes and gifts during the last twelve days before Christmas. The gifts and notes have little clues as to who is sending them. This is Character B, who is admiring character A from afar. Character B hopes to spend Christmas with character A. Does character A know them well, not that well, or even not at all?— You decide. Create a heart-felt and warm Christmas story, with love that's developed while one person admires the other from afar with gifts. When Christmas arrives, allow it to be a beautiful one for these two people, as character A works out who it is and cupid strikes in time for the big day, and New Year's celebrations. Heat and steam as always are up to you, but this could make a lovely sweet and clean Christmas romance.

Story Outline:

4th August

Situation: Characters A and B had a terrible Christmas last year, for whatever reason you decide. Give them emotional conflicts for them both internally to overcome. This could be trust, learning to love, etc. They are thrown together this year when they meet at a Christmas dinner, that a mutual friend hosts. The party is out of town, and they both travel separately to the location. Once there, they meet. What happens? Give them a Christmas to remember! Heat and steam levels are up to you.

Story Outline:

5th August

Situation: Character A is new to the town, city or even country. You decide why and how they have arrived in this new location. Also decide where they are emotionally with love, and how they feel about it? It's the week before Christmas and they are winding down, ready for the holiday, but also a bit disappointed that they will be spending Christmas alone in this new location for the first time. The weather is terrible and they are devastated when their only company at home goes missing—their new kitten. It's found a couple of days before Christmas by the local vet (character B), who makes contact to say they have found it. Love blossoms over the holiday for these two. What happens, and why is the vet also single? Steam and heat levels are up to you.

Story Outline:

6th August

Situation: On Christmas Eve, character A's car breaks down in the harsh weather. Where are they going to or coming from? How do they plan to spend Christmas – they are single. An irresistible stranger comes to the rescue. What happens? Who is the stranger and how do these two end up with an unexpected romance, that blooms over the holiday? Heat and steam levels are up to you.

Story Outline

7th August

Situation: Character A is someone who works for the mail office, and they love everything to do with correspondence. They randomly sign up to a group they found out about via their work notice board, to exchange Christmas cards with strangers. Being a lover of correspondence, they sign up. What happens when they send and receive one Christmas card, from someone who appears to be just what they are looking for!? They receive a card and a heart-felt letter from character B, telling them exactly what they hope for, for the new year, and it's what Character A hopes for too. How does this love affair via exchange of Christmas cards develop? Heat and steam levels are up to you.

Story Outline:

8th August

Situation: Characters A and B have been engaged for three years. This is too long for Character A; they want to set the date for their wedding. What is holding character B back? In the run up to Christmas, they start to both reflect on where their relationship is going for the new year. Character A backs off and breaks off the engagement; why did they do this? Then something 'tragic' happens or there is a realisation for character B. They do a U-turn back towards character A, in the last twelve days leading up to Christmas. Character B has twelve days to get their partner back. They realise it's them they want, and they are ready to overcome whatever has been holding them back. Create a story that shows growth in these people, and love that's renewed make 'twelve days' key to the story! Heat and steam levels are up to you.

Story Outline:

9th August

People: Write a romance featuring two mature characters. Both of them have grown up children, who will spend Christmas away from them, or maybe one has none at all. Give them a story as to why they are alone. This year, they will have a lonely Christmas because of this. Their paths cross in a coffee shop a few days before Christmas. Why are they both there? And over this coffee they share, how does this lead to a Christmas that's a new experience, and unexpected lasting love for these two mature characters? Heat and steam levels are up to you.

Story Outline:

10th August

Situation: Let's write a romantic comedy. A bride-to-be wants to have the perfect Christmas wedding, but something goes wrong in the run-up to her big day. She has just a few days to get it right. You decide how major the disaster is, give this a 'feel good' cute holiday theme that will leave readers fluffy inside! Heat and steam levels are up to you.

Story Outline:

11th August

Situation: On New Year's Eve, characters A and B cross paths in Time Square, New York, Paris, London or some major city where celebrations are held to see in the new year. What happens? Why are they there? Who are they with? Where are they going to or coming from? Give them a backstory or conflict they are dealing with, then turn their random meeting into a love affair that's starts off the new year. Heat and steam levels are up to you.

Story Outline:

12th August

Situation: New Year's Eve and the count-down is about to happen shortly. Character A feels disappointed that they've had another year without finding love. They decide to take a walk and go to get their favourite Chinese food, before they return home to celebrate on their own. Low and behold, they save a woman who is being robbed in an alley. What happens next? Where was she going? Who is she? And how does this 'fated' encounter turn into a love affair? Heat and steam levels are up to you.

Story Outline:

13th August

Situation: Character A has just landed in Hong Kong, China during the celebrations for Chinese New Year. Why are they there? They go on a local guided tour of the city, the guide (character B) takes a fancy to them. Write a romance, set in this part of the world, between a local and a visitor who meet in this situation. How does their love affair develop while character A is in China? Does their romance last longer than their initial visit? Heat and steam levels are up to you, and do some all-important research on the location and the Chinese New Year traditions.

Story Outline:

14th August

People: Character A is a wife whose husband has been away in the army. He is set to return home just before Christmas. Sadly, he does not make it home. What happens to him? While she's in mourning, she goes to a grief group to help deal with her loss. Here she crosses paths with Character B, who is not a member of the group but is the person who organises it. Give character B their own backstory that tells what made them start the group, or work for the organisation that manages it. With each week that she attends, the attraction builds! Tell their story, one where love is found after loss on both sides. Heat and steam levels are up to you.

Story Outline:

15th August

People: Character A is an aspiring romance author. Give her a day job, as well. She often sits and people watches in parks, cafes, etc. to get inspiration. A few times, she has seen Mr. Tall Dark and Handsome at the same spot. She has started to write him as a character into her short stories, from what she has noticed about him. Two days before Christmas, he approaches her. What does he say and where does this lead? Heat and steam levels are up to you.

Story Outline:

16th August

Situation: Write a story about a billionaire, or a very wealthy man seeking romance around Christmas. What does he do? Who does he cross paths with? He has been so busy throughout the year that he placed love on the bottom of his list. Now his hard work has paid off and he would love someone to spend the holiday with. He has had his eye on one of his female employees or a secretary for a while. What happens when he unexpectedly gifts her at Christmas? Heat and steam levels are up to you.

Story Outline:

17th August

Situation: Write a story about a four female friends who go away to a remote cabin for Christmas, it's a 'girls' trip.' One of them crosses paths with someone who shows great love interest—character B. How do they meet there? She's in a place where she is looking forward to the new year, and not really looking for love, but she can't resist him. Why is that? Who is he, what is he doing there? Does he work there or another guest? Heat and steam levels are up to you.

Story Outline:

18th August

People: New Year, new image, new me...What is changing for characters A and B when it comes to love and life? And how does this conflict with what they get, when they cross each other's paths?— you decide how this happens. However, they end up unable to leave each other alone. Heat and steam levels are up to you.

Story Outline:

19th August

People: Character A is 'anti-Christmas.' They hate everything about it. Why is this? As the preparations for Christmas get underway at their work office, a new co-worker (character B) who is full of Christmas cheer tries to get them in the spirit. What happens and how do they end up celebrating together? Bring character A on a U-turn back from their cynical self, and ready to start the New Year with character B. Heat and steam levels are up to you.

Story Outline:

20th August

People: She's attached or emotionally unavailable, he's not, but yet he is convinced that it's him she should be with this Christmas. How do they know each other? What is their history or backstory together? Create a Christmas love story with lots of warm feelings of love, as he pursues her. Allow your readers to go 'ahh how lovely.' Heat and steam levels are up to you.

Story Outline:

21st August

Situation: Character A is in the Army and they are returning home for Christmas. They have no significant other. However, as they return, they meet the love of their life. How do they meet? What happens when it's time to return to service? Heat and steam levels are up to you.

Story Outline:

22nd August

Situation: Characters A and B attend their old school reunion. They have both changed, but they were each other's first love. The reunion is just before Christmas. What happens when they meet again? How does romance spark? And why did they go their own separate ways originally? Heat and steam levels are up to you.

Story Outline:

23rd August

People: Character A has volunteered to help out at a food kitchen over Thanksgiving, or Christmas—you decide. Why have they done this? The food kitchen is for those in need and the homeless. This is their first time and while there, the kitchen owner— character B, has a backstory of their own. They were once homeless and in a bad state, they have recently managed to get back on their feet, then opened the food kitchen. How do these two develop a connection? What common ground do they share? Create a heart-felt, warm, loving holiday romance, with strong characters. Heat and steam levels are up to you.

Story Outline

24th August

Situation: 1950's Jazz scene. Your heroine is on stage singing a Christmas song, and looks drop dead gorgeous too. Your hero walks in and it's love at first sight from across the jazz lounge. How does he purse her in time for Christmas? How does this love affair start? Heat and steam levels are up to you.

Story Outline:

25th August

Situation: Christmas is coming up soon. In a small, remote town somewhere, there is a massive snowstorm and power outage. Character A ventures out to find help, Character B is a neighbour from a few miles away. When character B opens the door they welcome their neighbour, with open arms and safe place to stay. Character A hesitates, but takes some supplies and heads back home. Why do they hesitate? When the power cuts out again, Character B goes to check in on character A, as they know they are low on supplies. What happens next? Heat and steam levels are up to you.

Story Outline

26th August

People: Character A is a powerful, female CEO of a company. Her secretary has lined her up with a date for a Christmas event. This is because character A hasn't had time to find one, or even to date much. The man her secretary has lined up for her, is a silent partner in her competitor's business. She is not aware of this, until they have dinner to break the ice before the event. Do business and pleasure mix? He is keen on getting to know her more and tries to woo her; she remains guarded. How does he win her over? Create a story with strong, wealthy, characters who battle it out. In the end he wins her over for Christmas. Heat and steam levels are up to you.

Story Outline:

27th August

People: Write a story about a stressed, overworked single parent who finds love just in time for Christmas. Heat and steam levels are up to you.

Story Outline:

28th August

Situation: Character A bumps into character B on a plane just before Christmas; you decide where they are heading to. Character A is lucky to be on the flight as they had to switch for some reason to a later one. On the flight, character A is intrigued by character B. Once they land, what happens next? Create a 'fated' romance between these two. Heat and steam levels are up to you.

Story Outline:

29th August

Situation: Character A accidently picks up character B's bags at the airport; they have identical suitcases. What happens when they realise this, and character A contacts character B via the contact details on the luggage label? Heat and steam levels are up to you.

Story Outline:

30th August

People: character A and character B are both going for the same position at work. They have been trying to out-do each other all year professionally. Character A has enough and finds a new job just before Christmas, and is about to leave the company. Secretly character B has been fighting their own feelings over character A. Now they are about to leave the company, what happens? Can character B deal with them leaving on a bad note, and even worse leaving when they've had a thing for them for a while? Write an 'enemies to lovers' Christmas story. Heat and steam levels are up to you.

Story Outline:

31st August

Situation: Character A's personal journal has been left on the train or somewhere public. Character B finds it, reads it, and makes contact after searching on social media for the possible owner. What do they read in the journal? How do they feel? What makes them want to reach out at Christmas time? How does this turn into a whirlwind romance, where character B already feels like they know damn well that character A is the right person for them, from their diary entries alone? How does character A respond to their personal thoughts being read by another person? Heat and steam levels are up to you.

Story Outline:

September

Mixed Bag of Goodies

Welcome to September. From here on out you will have a 'mixed bag of goodies— all genres, and romance tropes. Pick and choose what grabs your creative taste buds and, as always, adjust the prompts to suit your genre, swap genders, and have a good play around.

1st September

Situation: Character A is a con artist of some sort. You decide exactly what he is up to. He's on a mission to pull off another one of his money-making deals. The person he is set to prey on, happens to be character B. Higher up the food chain those who give character A his orders never warned him, that character B is a woman, a beautiful one too! Once he learns all about her, does he pull off the scam, or do his feelings get in the way? What scam has he been allocated regarding character B also? Heat and steam levels are up to you.

Story Outline:

2nd September

Situation: Character A has just been released from jail, and has been assigned a probation officer. Their officer—character B, is stunning! Give character A a sinister past. Why were they in prison? How are they emotionally and mentally now they have been released back into society? Character B takes sympathy on them, and somehow in a twisty tale of 'forbidden love' lines are blurred between these two— you decide how, but make it page turning! Heat and steam levels are up to you.

Story Outline:

3rd September

Situation: Let's try a romantic crime thriller! Character A has been accused of a crime— you decide what kind of crime. Character B is aware that they are innocent. If they speak up, it will expose their love affair, but character B can't afford for it to be exposed. Why is this? What happens between these two? Also, how did their love affair start? What are the dangers involved? In the end what does character B do? Heat and steam level are up to you.

Story Outline:

4th September

People: Character A is from 'the wrong side of town.' Character B is from a wealthy background, or any contrasting background to character A's— you decide. Their paths cross when character B is at a place they should not be; their parents, family and friends would never approve. That said, they get to know one another in secret. Character A wants more, character B pulls away because of fear of disapproval over their connection to character A. How does character A convince B otherwise? What happens in this love affair? Heat, steam and suspense are up to you.

Story Outline:

5th September

People: Character A is a notorious drug lord at the top of the food chain, a man of wealth, style and intelligence as well as street smarts. He does not stand on street corners—he's the big boss at the top. However, he is trying to make enough money to leave it all behind him. That said, he has sworn off women—why is this? You decide his past. One woman has her eye on him; she feels he has a lot to offer a woman like her, a woman who craves the finer things in life. They cross paths somehow, you decide, and she tries to tame his heart and bring him around to loving her. Heat and steam levels are up to you. This could be a fantastic prompt for an urban romance also.

Story outline:

6th September

Situation: Character A is some form of law enforcement officer. They have been having a romantic affair with character B. Character B is placed as a suspect in a case they have been assigned. What is the case? What is the link to character B ? What happens? Heat, steam and suspense levels are up to you.

Story Outline:

7th September

Situation: Create a paranormal, Sci-Fi, supernatural or fantasy world in which character A is fighting for the good of their people—you decide what the fight is over or for. Within their 'clan' of people there is a rogue – character B—who just won't be tamed. They are against what the rest the clan is fighting for. They go as far as trying to stop, block, even remove or kill character A to keep them from achieving their goal. The characters don't really see eye to eye. Place something in character B's path that is unexpected. This allows them to have a change of heart. Character A is suspicious of their change of heart, but is pulled into them romantically somehow. Heat and steam levels are up to you.

Story Outline:

8th September

Situation: Character A has been dating Character B for some time and so far, things are going well. Until character A's ex turns up. What does the ex want? As far as Character B is concerned it ended on a bitter note and character A's ex left. Why did they leave? What does character A do? They thought they were no longer in love with the ex. Heat and steam levels are up to you.

Story Outline:

9th September

Situation: Today, let's write an inspirational romance. Your characters are both soul searching and trying to find the meaning of life. They each book themselves into some kind of retreat or weekend get-away, to get in touch with themselves. What challenges are they both facing? What has led them here? Allow them to find something in each other that they feel will help them move forward. They are both guarded with their hearts, but slowly this grip loosens. These two characters find love and become at peace with themselves. You can make this Christian romance, or even a contemporary one with the element of 'soul searching.' Heat and steam levels are up to you.

Story Outline:

10th September

People: Write a story about a lonely witch (a supernatural one in a made-up world or a human who practices magical arts), who is trying to find their soul mate. Character B is someone she 'enchants' and places a spell on. What happens, and how do they do this? How does their romance play out for the better or the worse? Heat and steam levels are up to you.

Story Outline:

11th September

Situation: Today is the anniversary of the sad terrorist attack in the USA. Today, let's write a story with an element of danger. Your main characters are in a location of your choice, and it catches fire or there is an 'alert' for safety. Everyone in the location needs to vacate, and fast. Character A is stuck and character B is aware that they are there. Against the advice of the emergency services, they race to assist them and get them out alive. Who are these characters? What are they doing in this location? Character A feels like they need to repay character B for saving their life; how do they do this and romance sparks? Both of these characters have their own individual challenges in their personal life they are dealing with— you decide what. However they become connected romantically via a tragic public state of emergency. Heat and steam levels are up to you.

Story Outline:

12th September

Situation: Character A wakes up in the woods. They are bruised and in slight pain. They can't recall what happened to them. They walk through this unfamiliar place, confused, and knock on the door of character B, who takes them in. Character A can't remember who they are, or what the hell happened. How does this situation play out for them? Who are these people, and what brings them together following this meeting? Heat, steam and suspense levels are up to you.

Story Outline:

13th September

People: Characters A and B are platonic friends; you place them into a situation where they have known each other for a while. They are both single and dating, however character A keeps making the same mistakes with love. Character B is their support through this. Character B feels they could offer character A what they are looking for in love, and wonders if their friendship could be more. How does character B suggest this or make their feelings known? Character A is not too sure about it, but somehow they decide to have a 'relationship trial' and see if it would work. Create a 'friends to lovers' story, with some tense moments for them both as they enter this new territory on a 'trial basis.' Heat and steam levels are up to you.

Story Outline:

14th September

Situation: Today I'd like you to think of your own love life and the experiences you've had. Pick situation where you've experienced a slight heartache. Rewrite this experience with an ending you would have loved. Change the people or keep them close to reality, if you like. Just rewrite this experience! Heat, steam, genre and suspense are all up to you.

Story Outline:

15th September

People: Today, think of a celebrity that you know of, or admire, who you know has had some ups and downs with love. Rewrite their story with a HEA! What happens? Heat, steam, genre and suspense levels are up to you.

Story Outline:

16th September

People: Today, draw on your friends for inspiration. Pick one who has had some ups and downs with love, or they have experienced something interesting when it comes to love. Rewrite their story. BUT, please, whatever you do, don't offend them! Today's prompt is to draw from real life experience around you and place your own spin on it. I suggest you change names etc... don't piss them off! Heat, genre, steam and suspense levels are up to you.

Story Outline:

17th September

People: Today, think of your ex! Create them as a character, improve them in a way you feel they may need, and rewrite them into a story. Create their journey to finding love after your relationship ended with them. Now… you could make this a romantic comedy and they end up the loser, or suffer heartache, or you can play nice— you decide. Heat, steam, suspense are all up to you.

Story Outline:

18th September

People: Character A is on their second divorce. What happened in their last two marriages? Now, they have sworn off love. Character B is someone from their past that they would have married if it was the right timing, but things didn't work out. Now, when they cross paths again (you decide how), does character A still feel the same way about marriage, when character B is clearly looking for a serious committed relationship? Create a love story with plenty of emotional investment and push and pull between the two. Give them a HEA that suits their individual growth as people, from their previous experiences with love and marriage. Heat and steam levels are up to you.

Story Outline:

19th September

Situation: Characters A and B are in a relationship. Character A has been working hard on their career and is starting to make some real progress. Character B feels that their career has 'changed them' somehow. They give character A an ultimatum 'me or the job.' What does character A do? If they break up in your story, allow some growth from character A. How do they realise that maybe what they had was worth holding on to? Heat and steam levels are up to you.

Story Outline:

20th September

People: Unlucky in love is today's theme. Write a story about character who just seems to have no luck with love, make it as tragic or as heart-felt as you want. Character A may even feel that they are jinxed or cursed. They find a love-interest—character B, in an unusual place, on a day when luck really does not seem to be on their side. It's one of the most unlucky days they've had for a while. Why is this? How do they meet? What happens here and who do they cross paths with? Create a HEA. Heat and steam are up to you.

Story Outline:

21st September

Situation: Character A has already ruled out character B as a
potential partner; they've said they'd never date someone 'like them
again', because of 'x, y, z.' You decide and fill in the gaps.
However, character B won't take no for an answer. How do they
bring character A on a U-turn so they agree to a date? What happens
on the date? Where does it lead? Create some push and pull, and lots
of tension! Heat and steam levels are up to you.

Story outline:

22nd September

Situation: Character A has a reputation with the opposite sex, one that scares off most of them. You decide what this is. Character B has heard about this, but it doesn't stop them from wanting character A. What happens between these two? What does character B do, and how does character A react? Heat and steam levels are up to you.

Story Outline:

23rd September

Situation: Characters A and B go away for a work conference; they work for separate companies. When they lock eyes across the conference room it's 'insta connection.' What happens while they are away for two days at the work conference? Heat and steam levels are up to you.

Story Outline:

24th September

Situation: Character A's elderly parent is terminally ill. They fall for their parent's home help carer—character B. How does this happen? Create a heart-felt romance. Heat and steam levels are up to you.

Story Outline:

25th September

Situation: Today, write a really sweet and wholesome romance. Character A is from a small town. They own an ice cream store or any kind of store you wish them to. They 'cute meet' character B, who is from out of town, at the store. Character B visits the town for what reason? Why do they stop at the store? Keep it sweet, clean, wholesome…and good luck! I probably could never do it.

Story Outline:

26th September

Situation: Let's write a really steamy or even erotic story today. Character A and character B meet, it's 'insta connection' and a one night steamy affair! What happens? And how does this progress to more than one night?

Story Outline:

27th September

Situation: Character A is a nude model for art students. One student—character B, has their eye on character A. They cross paths outside of the art class. Where? How? When? And what happens? Create a romance between these two that causes character A to rethink their job as a nude model, now that character B has their sights set on them. Heat and steam levels are up to you.

Story outline:

28th September

Situation: Create a 'right person, wrong timing' story. Characters A and B are perfect for each other – why is this? And how and when did they realise this? For both of them, there is something in the way a situation, person or thing that blocks their love at this moment in time. How do they handle it? Do they meet again later and what happens? Heat and steam levels are up to you.

Story Outline:

29th September

Situation: Character A is typically a 'good girl.' What happens when character B— a 'bad boy', crosses her path and sweeps her off her feet? How do they meet? Why does she try to avoid him at first, before he goes all out romantically to woo her? Allow character A to be just what character B needs in his life, even if he's not an angel. Heat and steam levels are up to you.

Story Outline:

30th September

People: Character A and Character B find each other via a salsa class they both take. What happens? How does one dance lead to love? Give them both their own individual challenges and hang ups but bring them on a U-turn towards love and romance together. Heat and steam levels are up to you.

Story Outline:

Romance Writers' Blogging Challenge

Month One- October

Welcome to October. Here we will take a look at the benefits of blogging and not just writing fictional romance. When I first became a published author, I started a blog or 'author site' as I heard 'that's what authors do.' I had no real idea what I was doing, what to write about or why I was doing it. But I soon learned that there are so many benefits to writing blogs, that are not always related to books or marketing on your own dedicated space. I started out on WordPress and highly recommend it if you don't yet have an author site. If you do, then I recommend that you start to make use of it! I found that:

1. I gained lots of followers to my blog, who really want to know about me as well as my work.
2. I met some wonderful other bloggers and authors. In fact, that's how I met my co-author.
3. It was just a wonderful way to be creative, allowing readers and potential readers to get to know the person behind the pen—me. If you're ever lucky enough to have a reader say, 'you're one of their favourite authors,' trust me, they would love to read your personal blog space too, as well as your books. So let's take a look. Here are some writing prompts outside of fiction for you to consider for your own personal author site or blog.

How do You Start Blogging? And How Often?

This is really down to you, but I recommend you try to do at least maybe one-three blogs of quality month, minimum. If you want to blog everyday so be it also, it's your space. I personally blog at last once a week, and have other featured authors on my blog, too. It's varied and busy on my blog site. Keep the blogs a reasonable length too. Mine, on average, are about 1,000-2000 words. I suggest you try to blog solidly for three months to see how your blog picks up, and hopefully gain new followers too. Here's some topics, you decide what grabs you. You don't need to work in any order, dip in and dip out.

- **1st October-** Today, let your readers know a little bit about you. What does your average day look like and what's your routine?
- **2nd October-** How did you start writing?
- **3rd October -**What drew you to the genre that you write?
- **4th October-** What's your favourite tense to write in—third person, first, past, present etc? What are your thoughts and experiences with writing in the present tense or even first person?
- **5th October-** Would you ever write in any other genre? Why or why not?
- **6th October-** What other authors inspire you and why? What author turned you into a bookworm or a writer?
- **7th October-** How do you feel about diversity in the romance genre, generally? How do you play your part to keep it diverse?
- **8th October-** Is there ever too much sex in romance? What's the difference between romance and erotica?
- **9th October-** What has been the most difficult scene or character for you to write to date? How did you overcome it, what were the challenges?
- **10th October-** In your view, is there any point in a prologue? Have used one or an epilogue?
- **11th October-** Where do you normally write? Describe your writing space.
- **12th October-** How do you handle negative reviews? What are your thoughts on less positive reviews generally?
- **13th October-** If you're a self-published author, what gems of wisdom do you have about the process?
- **14th October-** What's your pet peeve in romance stories, and why?
- **15th October-** Where do you get most of your writing inspiration? (Hopefully, I'm one LOL).
- **16th October-** Write a book review for the last book you really loved or one you didn't love.

- **19th October-** During the year 2020, we had a world-wide health pandemic, Covid-19. How did you spend your period of 'lock down?' Did it inspire you to become creative?
  20th October- How often do you write, and how do you balance it with work, family, your day-to-day routine, etc?
- **21st October-** What other hobbies do you have, what else do you enjoy?
- **22nd October-** Where did you grow up? Tell us about your travel experiences. Or where you'd love to travel to and why?
- **23rd October-** What's your biggest goal as a writer? Put it out to the universe!
- **24th October-** Are you a 'plotter or a panster' when you plan out story outlines? Share your approach.
- **25th October-** What advice would you give to an aspiring writer?
- **26th October-** What book made you cry, and why?
- **27th October-** What's your favourite romance trope to read and to write?
- **28th October-** What's your favourite season of the year: spring, summer, autumn or winter?
- **29th October-** How much does research play a role in your writing process?
- **30th October-** As a reader, what do you prefer—audio, e-book or paperbacks?
- **31st October-** How will you spend Halloween? Do you celebrate it at all or not? Why? (If you're not writing this around Halloween, you can still give your thoughts on the day).

Romance Writers' Blogging Challenge

Month Two- November

Welcome to November! So we'll continue our second month of the personal blog challenge, and hopefully by now if you've been consistent your readers have gotten to know you more, and you may hopefully have some new followers. If you don't have new followers yet, just keep going. They will come; I promise. And remember to be authentically you when you blog. Let's go.

- **1st November-** What lesson have you learned in life, the hard way?
- **2nd November-** Tell us about your English teacher in school. Did you get on with them, did you even like English?
- **3rd November-** What do you love about love? You're a romance writer after all, what do you call 'true love'? Have you found it?
- **4th November-** Write a letter to your eighteen-year-old self.
- **5th November-** How will you spend bonfire night/ or Guy Fawkes night ? Google search if you've never heard of it or need clarity. (If you're writing this around then only, if not you can still give your thoughts on this event).
- **6th November-** Write a letter to someone who really annoyed you, so you can get it off your chest! (Leave their name out).
- **7th November-** What are your views on the world right now? Look at the local news and headlines; what's your honest POV on all that's going on right now?
- **8th November-** What do you think is the biggest assumption people make about being a writer?
- **9th November-** What do you think is the biggest assumption people make about you, personally?
- **10th November-** How old were you and what were you doing when the year 2000 came around? How was your life? Your writing? Your ambitions and goals? What were they at this time?

- **11th November-** It's Veteran's Day, do you know anyone in the army? Do you think you could serve in the army? (If you're not writing on this day you can still give your thoughts on it.)
- **12th November-** Interview one of your fictional characters from your books.
- **13th November-** What's your guilty pleasure in life?
- **14th November-** What's the best and worst job you've ever had, and why?
- **15th November-** Grab a dictionary, open it up randomly, and point to a word. Write a post inspired by or about that particular word.
- **16th November-** Finish this scene 'as soon as he/she locked eyes with me I...?'
- **17th November** – What's harder for you to do, apologise, ask for help, or admit you're in love?
- **18th November-** What's one thing you are 'sorry not sorry' about? Be brutally honest about something you refuse to be sorry for!
- **19th November-** Are you a good cook? Share the recipe for something you can make really well. If you don't like cooking, tell us why.
- **20th November-** Are you a bold extrovert or more introverted? Why are you more naturally like this as a person?
- **21st November-** What's been the most interesting book you've read this year?
- **22nd November-** Black Friday today. What are your thoughts, experiences, feelings on this holiday? Do you plan to shop? Have you found any good deals? Are any of your books on offer for Black Friday? (Only relevant if you are writing this in November, if not generally how do you feel about the meaning and celebration of Black Friday?)
- **23rd November-** It's Thanksgiving in the USA. Write a blog post about gratitude what are you truly thankful for

right now. Do you celebrate this holiday or not? If so, what are your plans? (Only relevant if you are writing this in November.) If not, write a gratitude post today anyway!

- **24th November-** Write a poem today and share it.
- **25th November-** What animal would describe your personality and why?
- **26th November-** Reflect on this year so far. What have you achieved or not achieved as yet? How far off are you?
- **27th November-** What do you love about your city or town? Write a blog post as if you were a travel guide around the location. What is there to see and do?
- **28th November-** Do you still use the library these days? Do you think the library has a role in society given the changes with audio and e-books?
- **29th November-** What are some of your favourite movies and why? What do you love about them? Also, what music do you enjoy?
- **30th November-** Describe your dream home. Are you a city, small town, urban or suburbs kinda person? House or apartment?

Romance Writers' Blogging Challenge

Month Three- December

Welcome to December, the final month of the three-month blog challenge! Here are some topics to discuss on your author site to connect yourself with your audience, readers, followers and those who are just interested in you the romance author! Share them on social media also to reach people!

- **1st December-** Write a tiny piece of flash fiction today. Make it a short story of no more than, say,1,000 words.
- **2nd December-** What made you smile this week? Anything in the news, family, friends? Talk about anything at all.
- **3rd December-** When you were twenty one years old you were…
- **4th December-** Beach, forest, mountains ? Which location is best for you and why?
- **5th December-** Write about the last country you visited and why you'll never forget your time there.
- **6th December-** What is your perfect Saturday or Sunday? How do you spend the weekends?
- **7th December-** Can you play a musical instrument? If not, what instrument do you enjoy listening to and why? Which one would you love to play?
- **8th December-** If money were no object you'd….
- **9th December-** What is the one thing you would change about the world right now?
- **10th December-** Do you recycle? And what are your thoughts on second hand, charity or thrift stores? Have you ever been, and do you like them?
- **11th December-** Write a poem, blog, article, anything you want, inspired by the word 'butterfly.'
- **12th December-** Write a poem, blog, article, anything you wish, with inspiration from the word 'ambition.'
- **13th December-** Can you speak a second language? If so, how did you learn this and for what purpose? If you don't speak a second language what language appeals to you and why?

- **14th December-** What star sign are you? And what parts of this star sign's 'traits or reputation' are true and false for you personally.
- **15th December-** Write a blog post about something that is really important to you right now. This could be a cause, charity, issue, trend, whatever. Just write! Whatever pulls at your heartstrings, let us know.
- **16th December-** What do you see as a problem in the world right now? What's your honest, unapologetic solution to it?
- **17th December-** Finish this sentence: 'Two things I am not as a person is x and y, don't get me fucked up!' Write a blog post in detail, explain yourself!
- **18th December-** One thing you'll never create, feature, use or write about in your fiction work is... and why?
- **19th December-** What have you learned about the use of social media? How often do you use it and what for?
- **20th December-** What era or generation would you have loved to grow up in, lived in, or feel really drawn to and why?
- **21st December-** Write about your day today. How did it go?
- **22nd December-** Write about the writing projects you are working on at the moment.
- **23rd December-** What's your advice, POV or experience with dealing with a broken heart? In fact write an open letter to someone who broke your heart, explaining how and what you would have changed.
- **24th December-** If you were to come with a warning sign, what would it say!?
- **25th December-** What attracts you to the opposite sex (or even the same sex) and why?
- **26th December-** Are you team player or team leader?
- **27th December-** Give your readers five of your top tips to stay organised and motivated in life.

- **28th December-** Write a poem, article, blog, whatever with inspiration from the world 'inspiration.' Or who/what is your inspiration in life that keeps you going?
- **29th December-** Go to your window, describe what you see outside. If it's uninteresting, what would be the perfect view from a window for you?
- **30th December-** Are you a morning, evening, afternoon or late-night person? When are you at your best in the day?
- **31st December-** Do you have a beauty routine? What's your thoughts on the beauty industry?

Well done writer! I hope you've had a very productive 365 days. I really hope that this writing prompt book has helped to inspire you. If you enjoy it or have found something positive and motivational please do leave a review on Amazon or wherever you got your copy. I'd appreciate it. Even a short one will do. Happy writing.

Connect with me on social media here
Bookbub- www.bookbub/kimknight
Facebook- @kimknightauthoruk
Twitter- @kimknightauthor
Author site- www.kimknightauthor.com

Printed in Great Britain
by Amazon

53922009R00179